ALSO BY MICHELINE MAYNARD

City Tips: A Journalist's Guide to the World's Great Cities

The Selling of the American Economy :
How Foreign Companies Are Remaking the American Dream

The End of Detroit: How the Big Three Lost Their Grip on
the American Car Market

The Global Manufacturing Vanguard:
New Rules from the Industry Elite

Collision Course: Inside the Battle for General Motors

SATISFACTION GUARANTEED

HOW ZINGERMAN'S BUILT A CORNER DELI INTO A GLOBAL FOOD COMMUNITY

MICHELINE MAYNARD

SCRIBNER

New York London Toronto Sydney New Delhi

SCRIBNER

An Imprint of Simon & Schuster, Inc.
1230 Avenue of the Americas
New York, NY 10020

First Scribner hardcover edition February 2022

SCRIBNER and design are registered trademarks of The Gale Group, Inc., used under license by Simon & Schuster, Inc., the publisher of this work.

For information about special discounts for bulk purchases, please contact Simon & Schuster Special Sales at 1-866-506-1949 or business@simonandschuster.com.

The Simon & Schuster Speakers Bureau can bring authors to your live event. For more information or to book an event, contact the Simon & Schuster Speakers Bureau at 1-866-248-3049 or visit our website at www.simonspeakers.com.

Interior design by Alexis Minieri

Manufactured in the United States of America

1   3   5   7   9   10   8   6   4   2

Library of Congress Cataloging-in-Publication Data
Names: Maynard, Micheline, author.
Title: Satisfaction guaranteed : how Zingerman's built a corner deli into a global food community / Micheline Maynard.
Description: New York, NY : Scribner, 2022. | Includes bibliographical references.
Identifiers: LCCN 2021043170 (print) | LCCN 2021043171 (ebook) | ISBN 9781982164614 (hardcover) | ISBN 9781982164638 (ebook)
Subjects: LCSH: Zingerman's Community of Businesses. | Food industry and trade—Michigan—Ann Arbor—History. | Delicatessens—Michigan—Ann Arbor—History.
Classification: LCC HD9009.Z56 M39 2022 (print) | LCC HD9009.Z56 (ebook) | DDC 338.4/764795—dc23
LC record available at https://lccn.loc.gov/2021043170
LC ebook record available at https://lccn.loc.gov/2021043171

ISBN 978-1-9821-6461-4
ISBN 978-1-9821-6463-8 (ebook)

To everyone who taught me to cook

Contents

Introduction

The past few years have been devastating for the specialty food business. In the boom times of the late-twentieth century and into the twenty-first, prestigious shops and luxurious chains were able to convince customers to willingly part with tens or hundreds of dollars for a few minutes of pleasure. This was a world that made chefs and shop owners into celebrities, a world that bustled with innovation and flavors and drew consumers who avidly followed food trends.

Much of that seems to have evaporated, along with more than 110,000 restaurants that closed as COVID-19 swept the country. While it's tempting to blame the pandemic for their demise, the downward spiral began well before the pandemic spread across the United States.

Dean & Deluca, whose name was synonymous with expensive food, has disappeared. New York's beloved Fairway Markets filed for bankruptcy. Macy's, whose housewares filled countless kitchens and whose classrooms hosted countless chefs, is a fraction of its former size. Williams Sonoma shops have closed. So have Sur La Table stores. Family-owned places in cities all over the country vanished as younger generations decided not to carry on their parents' business. High rents drove some out of business; others simply couldn't find the employees they needed.

Layer COVID on top of that, and you have an industry that's

plummeted from the pedestal it once enjoyed standing on into an existential crisis. But as many restaurants and food purveyors have dealt with their demise, one company has survived and thrived: Zingerman's of Ann Arbor, Michigan.

In 2022, Zingerman's celebrates its fortieth anniversary, growing from a single crowded corner deli in a leafy college town to a $65 million business, with a vast following around the globe. More than two million people are on the mailing list for its catalogs, which overflow with quirky drawings, anecdotes about people who created the food, and mouthwatering descriptions. But Zingerman's means different things to different people.

To many customers, Zingerman's is food, such as the overstuffed sandwiches that first made the Deli famous, and the crusty bread, flavorful gelato, and hearty coffee that it produces in an industrial park on the south side of Ann Arbor. "It's like the Jewish deli on the hill," says Alon Shaya, a James Beard Award–winning chef with restaurants in New Orleans and Denver, known for his Israeli-inspired cuisine. "It's the one we all kind of look up to." Zingerman's contributed to the craze for balsamic vinegar, artisanal olive oil, and exotic spices from all over the world, long before they were widely available. Shoppers can buy them in person at the Deli or via Mail Order, which sent out its first hand-drawn catalog nearly thirty years ago.

About half the items in the catalog are made by Zingerman's, but the other half are from specialty food companies that Zingerman's has helped establish among food lovers, like Nueske's, the admired Wisconsin maker of cured meats, Benton's, famous for its Tennessee bacon, and American Spoon from northern Michigan, a source of fruit spreads and sauces. Says Ethné de Vienne, owner of Épices de Cru in Montreal, whose spices fill two displays in the Deli, "Nobody is as dynamic or like-minded to us as Zingerman's."

Within the business world, however, Zingerman's is known as a valuable resource of management ideas, which its cofounders, Paul Saginaw and Ari Weinzweig, have taught to leaders in and outside the food world. Celebrated chefs Rick Bayless of Chicago and Joanne Chang of Boston have turned to Zingerman's for advice in both leadership and staff training. Through the years, Ti Martin, co-owner of Commander's Palace in New Orleans, has studied and relied upon Zingerman's techniques for good service and transparent finances. "I don't know which ones I stole from Ari and which I made up myself," she says of Weinzweig. Like Zingerman's, she believes that "growth is a good thing, but it's why you want to grow that matters."

Millennial entrepreneur Kat Gordon of Muddy's Bake Shop in Memphis regularly practices the lessons she learned from ZingTrain, the business that provides training to both Zingerman's staff and outsiders who wish to learn the company's management techniques. In 2021, Gordon renovated her bakery to include a classroom where she conducts a class in "Visioning," one of the company's basic concepts. In it, participants craft a picture of what they'd like their business or their personal lives to look like in the future. "I'm a better business owner, and a better manager and a better human, for having had anything to do with ZingTrain," Gordon says.

Zingerman's has provided a stage for hundreds of food celebrities in the special dinners it holds at the Roadhouse, its flagship sit-down restaurant, and in the pastry classes at Bake!, which have featured cookbook writers Dorie Greenspan and Stella Parks. It takes part in countless community fund-raisers, some benefiting its own charity, Food Gatherers, which collects millions of pounds of unused food from restaurants and stores in Ann Arbor and redistributes it to people in need. For the past decade, save for a pandemic break, Zingerman's drew attendees from around the world to Camp Bacon, its annual pork-centered symposium looking at history and evolving trends.

Zingerman's customers include Barack Obama, Oprah Winfrey, and

Maria Shriver, as well as countless food lovers, including generations of University of Michigan students (and their parents) who provide Zingerman's with a constant flow of new people to please. Collectively, its approach has made it an entrepreneurial superstar—"the coolest company in America," according to *Inc.* magazine—even as much older and more prestigious names dissolve. Zingerman's is a successful survivor because it was fundamentally strong, allowing it to withstand the pandemic and get back on its feet.

WHY ARE ZINGERMAN'S CUSTOMERS SO HAPPY?

On the website for Zingerman's Mail Order business, you'll find a return policy that sums up the company's approach to business.

THE ENTIRE EXPERIENCE COUNTS

Our guarantee doesn't just cover food. We ensure your satisfaction with every part of your experience with Zingerman's. From picking up the phone, to the first mouse click on your computer, until you finish the last bite of bread—if you aren't completely satisfied with every part of the journey please contact us. We want to hear about the problem. We'd love the opportunity to make you happy.

This satisfaction-guaranteed philosophy has been Zingerman's approach since its founders opened the Deli's doors in 1982. "They wanted to bring value in more than one dimension," says Steve Wallag-Muno, one of Zingerman's original employees, who created its lively logo and the look of its illustrations.

At Zingerman's, I see smaller-scale similarities with some of the world's most successful companies, especially Toyota, which I've written about for publications such as the *New York Times, Fortune*, and *Forbes*. It's no accident. In the earliest years of the company, Zingerman's cofounders were voracious readers of business books, looking for management tips that they could apply at the Deli. Zingerman's has been directly influenced by Toyota's philosophy of *kaizen*—continuous improvement and visual management, meaning that it's easy to see at a glance the type of work that needs to be done.

As at Toyota, the training that new employees receive and the topics they are expected to master at Zingerman's are clearly stated during their first week, and there is ample opportunity for employees to make suggestions that will help Zingerman's improve its service and finances. Like Toyota, whose subsidiary companies produce a significant share of its auto parts, Zingerman's also relies on vertical integration. Products produced by Zingerman's go into the menu items at the Deli, the Bakehouse, and its restaurants, and are sold directly to Mail Order customers and as a wholesaler to other businesses. Toyota's concepts have even helped Mail Order solve its annual quandary in dealing with the surge in orders that takes place every holiday season.

ZINGERMAN'S THREE BOTTOM LINES

Zingerman's articulates its focus in a simple phrase: *great food, great service, and great finances.* It calls these its "three bottom lines," but Saginaw emphasizes that these are not the same as a traditional bottom line that reflects a company's profits. Like the legs of a stool, he says all three must be in balance for Zingerman's to be successful. Saginaw emphasizes that hitting financial goals is not the company's primary purpose, as it might be at a typical enterprise. "The reason you want to be successful is so you can continue the mission" of feeding customers and making them happy, he says. Zingerman's wants to achieve great "finances"—not "profits"—

because hitting a specific profit target is not its only priority. Zingerman's strives to be in the black so that it can invest in its businesses, share its prosperity with employees, and benefit the local community. This is Zingerman's essential "Why?"—the business idea popularized by Simon Sinek's 2009 TED talk and subsequent book, *Start with Why*, that a clear definition of purpose is essential to attracting customers and retaining staff.

Across Zingerman's, financial success isn't uniform. Although Saginaw and Weinzweig believed that each company should be self-sustaining, in reality, the most prosperous parts of Zingerman's, like Mail Order and the Bakehouse, shore up its smaller operations, such as the Creamery and Food Tours. The founders consider them important to the overall company, but they might not thrive as independent players in the tough food world. This loyalty to all its businesses, not just those generating the most revenue, is a reason Zingerman's routinely records minimal annual profits across the enterprise.

The slim-to-nonexistent profit margins, even in pre-pandemic times, at some Zingerman's businesses might be surprising, given the prices of its sandwiches, gourmet goods, and restaurant meals. After all, a single overstuffed sandwich costs close to twenty dollars. I can expect to spend thirty to forty dollars for a sit-down lunch at Zingerman's Roadhouse, and its most popular Mail Order gift boxes can cost a hundred dollars or more. Those prices can be polarizing, both in its hometown and elsewhere. But, as you read on, you'll understand that Zingerman's aims for a different type of prosperity. As Weinzweig explains, "Our bottom line is derived from customer satisfaction. We believe that giving great service is an honorable profession."

Along with many management tips, this book brings stories of the delicious food Zingerman's serves, from the bread, cookies, and coffee cakes that are turned out by the thousands at the Bakehouse, to the espresso and house-made candy bars, to the barbecue prepared daily at the Roadhouse. I'll explain the travel, tasting, testing, and experience that goes into selecting a tin of tuna for the Mail Order catalog or the recipe for hot cocoa cake that is one of Zingerman's most popular gifts.

WHAT YOU'LL TAKE HOME

Zingerman's ideas can be applied to whatever you do, whether your company is large or small, just as Toyota's philosophy has become familiar to everyone who studies business. You'll be hungry for the opportunity to use its ideas to make your work life—and your personal life—more joyful. You'll find out how Zingerman's employees have gone from jobs in the Deli to owning pieces of the company, the pleasure they get from working there, and why so many stay so long. Says Saginaw, "I don't buy into traditional economic theory that the business of business is business. What matters most to me is when my employees say that they work in a group with their friends. I could ask no more than that."

ZINGERMAN'S AND ME

As Zingerman's was born and grew in the 1980s and 1990s, I was building my career as a journalist, shuttling between Detroit, New York, Washington, and Tokyo. Wherever I went, people would ask where I was born. When I replied, "Ann Arbor," the reply would often be, "Oh, I went to Michigan" or "I know someone who went to Michigan." Around 2000, I began to hear people reply, "We love Zingerman's" just as often. As I got more interested in the topic of food, I started to see Zingerman's as a valuable resource. On my visits to the Deli, I'd look for the hand-lettered signs on big sheets of butcher paper that advertised the upcoming tasting classes, two-hour lessons devoted to the foods Zingerman's made or sold, or even just what its staff wanted to teach.

A class on coffee went deep into the roasting process and taught us how to pull a perfect espresso shot. A butter class let us taste different varieties from around the world, including cow, sheep, and goat. I took classes in chocolate, one in gelato, another on olive oil, studied the Mexican sauce mole, learned about Parmesan cheese, and in one session, we made fresh mozzarella.

At Bake!, the teaching arm of Zingerman's Bakehouse, I took classes in Italian cookies, flatbreads, and my biggest nemesis, pies. I don't know if other people cry in frustration when it comes to crust, but I did, and was soothed by Zingerman's instructors. My family and neighbors were gifted dozens of the results, but the biggest payoff was to my skill level.

With these classes under my belt, in 2007 I signed up to spend a week at the Paris cooking school run by Patricia Wells, the famed author and journalist best known for *The Food Lover's Guide to Paris*. Patricia's week-long classes are divided into a daily lecture and discussion portion and then a hands-on cooking lesson. She circulates through her teaching kitchens in Paris and Provence, observing and offering tips.

At the end of our first class, as my cooking partner and I were plating up the main course—harissa-spiced lamb—Patricia said, very quietly, "You can cook." I felt as if I'd been given the Legion of Honor, which Patricia wore to a lunch later in the week, and I knew Zingerman's deserved some of the credit for her compliment.

One day Patricia introduced us to an olive oil purveyor, and my classmates flocked into their tiny shop after class to buy canisters to take home. A few weeks later, I was browsing olive oil in Zingerman's Deli and spotted the same artisanal producer. I didn't have to go to Paris for it—the same product was in my backyard. Likewise, in London, I went into the Neal's Yard Dairy near Borough Market, armed with an introduction from Weinzweig. As I waited to meet one of the cheese mongers, I noticed a familiar yellow paperback for sale: the *Zingerman's Guide to Good Eating*.

I realized that Zingerman's, the little store on a street corner in a

Midwest college town, was the hub of a global wheel of food, and that the spokes extended around the world—to Montreal, where it selected spices from Épices de Cru in the Jean-Talon Market, to Costa Rica, where beans for Zingerman's Coffee are sourced, to England, for Montgomery cheddar and other cheeses, to Italy, for artisanal olive oil and the bags of pasta stacked on its shelves, and points all over America. "The role of a place like Zingerman's is incalculable, especially today, when so much of the world is about generic brands and chain food," says Richard Florida, best-selling author of *The Rise of the Creative Class*.

All that takes research, curiosity, resourcefulness, and passion, and it also takes convincing people that they should spend their money on Zingerman's products. That's always been a factor for Zingerman's, where the quality is high and the prices match. Michigan is regularly battered by fluctuations in the economy, suffering deeply in 2009, when two of its car companies went bankrupt. Even in wealthy Ann Arbor, largely shielded from economic cycles by the university, eyebrows still go up at the prices that Zingerman's charges, like rare balsamic vinegars that can cost $250 a bottle (and are kept in a locked glass case). I've experienced that sticker shock, too. In 2019, I spotted a bag of dried Italian pasta on the shelf for $19. *How could spaghetti be worth $19?* I wondered.

The prices are why Zingerman's can sometimes be a controversial topic. For example, after I got my second vaccine shot in March 2021, I went to the Roadhouse for a celebratory bowl of gumbo and posted a photo to Facebook, which prompted this response from a pal in England: "Were you given $1,000 for getting vaccinated in the U.S.?" No, I replied, puzzled. "I just thought you did," he went on, "because you could afford to go to Zingerman's afterward." That kind of reaction happens so frequently that Zingerman's has posted an essay on the Deli's website, explaining "Why our sandwich costs what it does." Its basic answer is, "Better food costs money."

After the hours I spent investigating every corner of Zingerman's businesses, I can tell you that your money buys you true handicraft. I watched teams of bakers loading racks of heavy Bundt pans into ovens, cake decorators individually sculpting edible flowers, and chefs following the seventeen steps needed to produce a single order of macaroni and cheese.

And Zingerman's doesn't sell only $19 pasta. There are options for $10 less. "Yes, but I'm still paying $9 for pasta," you might reply. What makes it different than $2.99 Barilla or De Cecco, or other widely available brands? The answer, basically, is that somebody made it, and it's likely that a Zingerman's managing partner has met that person and been to their fields, olive grove, or dairy. Before the word *artisanal* became commonly used in the late-twentieth-century food world, Zingerman's tracked down products made in small batches, not in big factories. It's that authenticity that connects the purveyor to the customer that is the foundation of Zingerman's brand character.

PART ONE

The Backstory

Zingerman's cofounders Paul Saginaw (*left*) and Ari Weinzweig in 1982.

(Courtesy of Ari Weinzweig)

CHAPTER ONE

Zingerman's Best Day—
and Its Worst

For the first thirty-eight years that Zingerman's was in business, Ari Weinzweig often began his mornings at the back table in Zingerman's Next Door, a tall yellow house in the Kerrytown section of Ann Arbor that Zingerman's converted into a coffee and candy shop, with indoor seating for customers from the adjacent Deli. Tall and lanky, deeply tanned, with glasses and a toothy smile, Weinzweig picked his spot, which became known as Ari's table, so he could watch everything that was happening in the café, and also see out to the courtyard and across to the Deli.

From that seat, Weinzweig, who cofounded Zingerman's in 1982, watched parents coaxing their children to take a bite of applesauce or macaroni and cheese. He viewed University of Michigan students splitting one of the Deli's gigantic sandwiches, and could glance around at local businesspeople gazing at their laptops, in between greeting customers who continuously stopped by, and while he was drafting a newsletter or working on his latest book.

In early spring 2014, Weinzweig saw something that seemed unusual in casual Ann Arbor: a clean-cut man in a suit, far more formally dressed than the typical Zingerman's visitor, especially at such an early hour. He watched the visitor slowly walk around the courtyard, peering in the door of the Deli. Intrigued, Weinzweig went outside to investigate. "Can I help you with anything?" he remembers asking. The man leaned toward him and said quietly, "Someone might be stopping by."

That someone was then-president Barack Obama.

The Obama visit was not a complete surprise. During his 2008 and 2012 presidential campaigns, Obama paid regular visits to Michigan, and while in office, he made a number of presidential appearances across the state, especially after the multibillion-dollar bailout that saved General Motors and Chrysler and preserved the state's manufacturing-focused economy. During one of those events, Zingerman's received an order for sandwiches from a member of the Secret Service. The agent arrived at the Deli to pick up his order, then brought the food to Air Force One, parked at Detroit Metropolitan Airport about thirty minutes away.

Weinzweig doesn't know if Obama had one of those particular sandwiches, but suspects he might have. After that trip, the Obama-Zingerman's relationship began to develop, both on the menu and in policy matters. On a subsequent trip, Zingerman's prepared a sandwich specifically for Obama to nosh. It named a gelato after him—Barack-y Road, a riff on Rocky Road—and created a pecan-topped cinnamon roll called an Obama Bun, all with White House approval (or at least without being told to cease and desist). Meanwhile, Saginaw, the business strategist to Weinzweig's management philosopher, became active in efforts to raise the state and federal minimum wage. Zingerman's already paid more than the Michigan minimum to employees, along with other benefits, but it advocated for other businesses to pay more. During the first Obama administration, Saginaw was invited to attend a White House conference on the topic, where he talked with the president and the first lady. He was subsequently the recipient of a Champions of Change Award, presented in a White House ceremony.

And now, on April 4, 2014, Obama himself was showing up.

Weinzweig had another event to attend that day, and logically turned hosting duties over to Saginaw. Late in the morning, police cars and Secret Service vehicles descended on the little cobblestone stretch of Detroit Street outside the Deli, blocking it off at both ends. Then came the motorcade, and Obama stepped out of the big SUV called the Beast, accompanied by Michigan congressman Gary Peters (now a U.S. senator). Saginaw welcomed them and watched as Obama went behind the cheese and meat counters, shaking hands and chatting with employees. The group then headed to the back of the Deli to order lunch. Obama, who had looked over Zingerman's lengthy menu on the ride over, told Saginaw he knew exactly what he wanted: sandwich No. 2, the Deli's famous Reuben, with a crunchy garlic pickle and a side of spinach salad. Peters joked that since Obama was paying, he'd have the same. And, in fact, Obama did pay. Knowing the first lady's emphasis on healthy eating, Saginaw expressed surprise at this sandwich order to a Secret Service agent, who said quietly, "When he's with Michelle, he orders a salad. When he's by himself, he gets what he wants."

You might wonder why the Reuben caught the president's attention. Here's what's on it: corned beef made for Zingerman's by Sy Ginsberg in Detroit; Swiss cheese from Switzerland; house-made Russian dressing; on Jewish rye baked in Zingerman's own bakery. That Reuben has been featured on the Food Network and called "the quintessential destination sandwich" by food critic John Lehndorff. (If you want to try it, Zingerman's Mail Order will sell you a kit so you can make one at home.)

Of course, a president's day isn't all play, and Obama's visit to the Deli included some work time. He met with three hourly workers from other restaurants, who were pushing for a higher minimum wage. He shook hands with diners who had been locked into the Deli for security purposes during his visit, and passersby who gathered outside as word of his presence there spread. And then came his endorsement. "The Reuben is killer," Obama later told a crowd at the University of Michigan. "I ordered a small and gave half to (presidential adviser and University of Michigan law school graduate) Valerie Jarrett, who traveled with us. And when I finished the half, I wanted the half back."

He continued, "I went there for two reasons. One is that the sandwiches are delicious. The other is that Zingerman's is a business that treats its employees well." Obama's quote about the Reuben is now painted on the wall of the Deli's dining room. "That was pretty nice," Saginaw recalls.

"THE WORST DAY OF MY LIFE"

Just six years later, Zingerman's was at its historic low as COVID-19 spread across the United States. The pandemic was a firestorm for the food business, which was suffering well before shutdowns were ordered in March 2020. More than 110,000 restaurants closed in the pandemic's first year, while others did a fraction of their normal business. Weinzweig was among those left shell-shocked. "This is the worst day of my life," he said during a phone call on Monday morning, March 16. "I just had to lay off three hundred people."

That day, Michigan governor Gretchen Whitmer issued a stay-at-home order that later made national news when armed protesters descended on the capitol building in Lansing, demanding she reopen the state. Still, many residents anticipated the order, since the governor of neighboring Ohio had declared a similar shutdown the previous weekend. On Sunday, March 15, I figured I had one last chance to eat at Zingerman's Roadhouse, the restaurant serving classic American food that has been part of Zingerman's Community of Businesses (ZCoB) since 2003.

I like to sit at a zinc-topped counter facing the kitchen, where I can wave to the chefs and chat with the hosts and my favorite servers. That

Sunday afternoon, I was the only customer at the counter, with just a handful of people at tables nearby. We all knew something was coming. Zingerman's was hardly alone in issuing layoff notices; by April 2020, an estimated 5.5 million restaurant employees would be thrown out of work. But it was a sea change for a company that had grown to $65 million in annual revenue. Right up until the stay-at-home order, Zingerman's was taking on new employees, says Amy Emberling, the managing partner at Zingerman's Bakehouse. The bread-and-pastry business, which has been around since 1994, was the first one founded after the original Deli.

Every week, Zingerman's sent out a lively email with the subject line "Zingerman's Is Hiring!" Despite its reputation as a place where people liked to work, and many stayed for decades, the constant flow of students in and out of Ann Arbor and the area's perpetually low unemployment rate, meant that Zingerman's, like every other local business, had to compete for employees. Its emails regularly listed jobs available in baking, candy making, the Mail Order business, catering, the restaurants, and more.

Within a week of the shutdown order, the partners in the Zingerman's businesses met in a socially distanced room to talk about what might happen. The outlook was bleak. Weinzweig estimates that overnight, Zingerman's annualized revenue fell by $20 million to about $45 million. Its catering business evaporated, weeks before the busy commencement and wedding seasons were about to start, affecting multiple businesses whose stories you'll read in this book. Its training program went from a lineup of daily in-person classes to nothing. All its food tours, a small but growing business, were canceled. As the Zingerman's businesses figured out their responses, the one exception to the gloom was the Mail Order business. It was inundated with orders from customers around the world who were avoiding grocery stores and stymied in their efforts to find quality food.

By summer, demand for items from the Zingerman's catalog, like bread, gelato, olive oil, vinegar, and candy, had grown by 100 percent. Eventually, by the end of its fiscal year in July, the entire Zingerman's

Community of Businesses clawed back to $63 million in annual revenue, only $2 million below fiscal 2019, and by 2021, it was back to $65 million. While some of its operations lost money, including the famous Deli, and continued to do so as the 2022 fiscal year kicked off, the red ink was offset by Zingerman's strongest performers and was not nearly as devastating as the sea that flooded the food world.

Nonetheless, the partners' meeting in March 2020 did not simply spell business as usual for Zingerman's. Emberling says each piece of the company was empowered to innovate. For Zingerman's, the pandemic was "like starting all over again," Emberling says. In the months that followed, ideas bubbled up across the businesses, some successful, some not, some of which became permanent, others dispensed with when employees found they did not work, or statewide restrictions were lifted, allowing them to fade away.

However, one theme resonated: The company's mantra of good food, good service, and good finances—at least, someday—remained intact. As the company rebuilt itself to prosper in a pandemic-shaken world, its philosophy did not change. In fact, says Weinzweig, Zingerman's guiding principles became the touchstones for its survival and the adjustments that followed. Without its accomplishments from 1982 onward, this book might be telling simply a history, and not a vision for the future. But Zingerman's has one, informed by its past.

THE CUSTOMER APPROACH

While Zingerman's is fundamentally a food business, producing its own and marketing others', its other hallmark is customer service. Weinzweig has devoted a book to that topic, but his philosophy boils down to a few basic tenets. The customer should be treated with respect, and the customer experience is not something to rush. Anyone who's shopped at the

Deli, or gone to the Bakehouse, knows that when their turn comes up, they have the clerk's full attention. If you ask about wildflower honey, you aren't just pointed to an aisle. Someone walks you to it and tells you about its characteristics. There also isn't any real pressure to buy. If you're on a learning expedition, that's fine. If you're buying hundreds of dollars of food items, all the better.

I've never taken anyone to Zingerman's who wasn't impressed by something, whether it's the service or the food or simply the atmosphere. So much effort goes into creating the experience for those customers. Each staffer who comes in contact with the public is given extensive training from the first moment they clock in, and by the end of their first week, they have received more instruction than many retail workers get in a career. The lessons go on for weeks, months, and years, often bolstered by travel to Italy, Ireland, and elsewhere in Europe; as well as countries in Central and South America, such as Costa Rica and Brazil; and Africa, such as Ethiopia and Morocco. There are opportunities to rise from making sandwiches to becoming an executive chef. And some receive the inspiration to start businesses of their own.

Zingerman's takes an innovative approach to new foods, business policies, and concepts shared across the company. And it starts with two men—Weinzweig and Saginaw—who went to the University of Michigan and had a meeting of minds that made food business history.

CHAPTER TWO

How the Deli Came to Life

When you drive along Fourth Avenue in downtown Ann Arbor, you'll see a branch of the Ruth's Chris Steakhouse chain, with the familiar red-and-white neon sign that decorates a hundred similar locations around the country. But this branch of Ruth's Chris merits a historic marker, and not only because it was once an Edsel dealership. It's where the seeds for Zingerman's Deli were planted.

In the late 1970s and early 1980s, this building housed Maude's, a contemporary American café that was part of a local restaurant group called Mainstreet Ventures (the name came from Ann Arbor's own Main Street, a block west). It was founded by the late Dennis Serras, whose establishments dominated the downtown restaurant scene. In a college town replete with vintage bars, Greek restaurants, and casual places, Maude's seemed hipper and more modern. It was the type of place that would have fit into a lively Chicago neighborhood. Teens like me didn't put up a fuss when our parents wanted to eat there. Sometimes, we even went to Maude's on our own with friends.

In the 1970s, the manager at Maude's was Paul Saginaw. He'd been a bartender at another Mainstreet Ventures restaurant, the Real Seafood Company, which still operates on Main Street. Saginaw was born and

11

raised in Detroit, and his Jewish parents joined the exodus of white families leaving the city after the 1967 riots, with Paul finishing high school in suburban Southfield. Saginaw fell in love with food early on, frequenting the area's Jewish delis, with their big, fat sandwiches stuffed with corned beef, and the glass cases full of side dishes like potato salad and coleslaw. (He also inherited a love of gambling from his uncle, who took him to Las Vegas at a young age, prompting him to vow that he'd live there someday.)

At Maude's, Saginaw frequently hired students from the University of Michigan who came looking for jobs to help pay their way through school. One student was Ari Weinzweig, a Russian Studies major, who had also been exposed to Jewish deli food growing up in Chicago. He had no restaurant background, but that didn't matter to Saginaw, who was used to training rookies. Many of the student hires disappeared after graduation, but Weinzweig was enthusiastic about his work, coming up with ideas far beyond his job description. For instance, he recommended that Maude's put a sandwich on its menu called the Georgia Reuben, a riff on the original that substituted turkey and coleslaw for corned beef and sauerkraut.

The young men were a few years apart in age—Saginaw was born in 1951, Weinzweig in 1956—but shared an appreciation for the other dishes that delis were famous for, like latkes with applesauce, bagels, and knishes—easy to find in the big cities, but less common in Ann Arbor, despite a sizable Jewish community. Michigan earned the derisive nickname "Jew U" in the 1920s, for welcoming Jewish students when Ivy League and other private schools imposed quotas on admissions. Today, about 15 percent of the school's fifty thousand students are Jewish.

When Saginaw and Weinzweig arrived in the 1970s, however, they felt Ann Arbor was missing something essential. Sure, you could buy bagels on Sundays at the Blue Front, a corner store near the Michigan campus that also sold halvah and other Jewish treats. However, the bagels had to be brought in from Detroit in big brown paper bags, and if you didn't snap yours up by noon, they were gone. Likewise, Ann Arbor lacked the hearty rye and pumpernickel breads that Weinzweig grew up with in Chicago. There was no consistent local source for good deli meat, like pastrami and corned beef. At that time in Ann Arbor, before good grocery stores had deli counters, you were pretty much limited to prepackaged versions.

Saginaw and Weinzweig agreed that Ann Arbor needed a good deli. And they both were interested in running one someday. But a plan took a while to develop. Weinzweig left Ann Arbor for a time, while Saginaw received a compelling opportunity—Serras offered him the chance to become a partner in Mainstreet Ventures. Saginaw discussed it with his wife, Lori, and decided to take out a second mortgage on their home to come up with the capital required to join the owners. But the decision made him uneasy. Although Mainstreet's restaurants were prosperous, Saginaw felt they put too much emphasis on volume, not on satisfying individual customers.

An unexpected alternative arose. Saginaw's friend Mike Monahan came to him with the idea of buying the fish market that Real Seafood operated in the Kerrytown Market Building, a few blocks north of downtown. If you walk into Kerrytown now, it looks like a scene set in a Nancy Meyers movie. There are young people running food stands, aisles of bountiful produce, a meat market, a wineshop, a coffee place, and a store selling electric bicycles. You can hear notes from a carillon and find yarn, spices, and a store specializing in olive oil. Outside, there's a bustling farmer's market on Saturdays year-round, and on Wednesdays, too, from May to December. Both attract locals, chefs, students from Community High School nearby, and visitors, especially on football Saturdays.

But in the late 1960s, the market area was scruffy. It became the centerpiece of an effort by a dozen local businessmen to encourage investment in the Kerrytown district. Monahan was excited by the opportunity to help elevate the area, and Saginaw knew that he had piscatorial chops. "Mike knew everything about fish," Saginaw recalls. Convinced by Monahan's enthusiasm, Saginaw instead used the money from his second mortgage to finance Monahan's Seafood Market. It opened in 1978, and remains in business, serving lunch daily and selling all kinds of high-quality fish, like Cooper River King Salmon during its short season, and jumbo shrimp from the Louisiana Gulf Coast. Back then, they had the fish business to themselves. "We opened when there wasn't any fresh fish around," Saginaw says. "We were the first ones in the area to have sashimi-quality fish, and I was fearless with all kinds of weird things. Fish was a lot cheaper back them."

The idea was a success. In 1981, the three-hundred-square-foot stand did more than $1 million in business, including the fish it sold to area restaurants. Monahan and Saginaw would receive whole fish from their vendors, then gut, scale, fillet, and display them on ice. For a time, Saginaw was ecstatic about his decision. "Here I am, in this fish market, really happy," he says. "It was small, and if you wanted to have a perfect day, it was within your power to make it happen. I'm not going into the restaurant; I'm not dealing with drunks at two a.m."

"Paul was a businessman," Monahan remembers, "so it was kind of a nice complementary relationship. I learned a lot from him about business. And he learned a lot from me about fish. And we both learned what the hell we were doing because we were young." Then they made a mistake. The pair opened a second fish market in Farmington Hills, Michigan, about a thirty-minute drive away. They sent their friend Frank Carollo, an engineering graduate from Michigan who had worked at Maude's, to run it. But the Farmington Hills fish market sat across the street from a vast Kroger grocery store, which had its own fish counter, and constant deals that made it difficult to compete. The complexities of managing two fish stores that were not close together became unwieldy. It was clear that the second fish venture was doomed.

Simultaneously, the dream of a deli still lingered. Two blocks away from Kerrytown sat a little brick store, built in 1902, at the corner of Detroit and East Kingsley Streets. Originally called Disderide's grocery, the building was owned by Arthur Carpenter, who had been part of the Kerrytown development group. Called The Marketplace—A Delicatessen, it served its customers cafeteria style. Saginaw wasn't impressed with the food, and the diners weren't, either. Business dwindled, and Carpenter decided to close the deli after owning it for less than a year.

In the winter of 1982, Carpenter dropped in to see Saginaw at Monahan's. He offered him a lease on the building, with all the equipment included. Saginaw and Monahan talked briefly about moving the fish market there but decided that was too complicated. "We were really trying to keep it together and grow, and my heart was with the fish," Monahan says. "Those guys have that Jewish deli background, and I wasn't really interested in that business." But Monahan and his wife agreed to make an investment, and help Saginaw get his business off the ground.

On a chilly Sunday morning, Saginaw went to Weinzweig's house and woke him up. "I've found a location for us to open that delicatessen we've been talking about," he said. They calculated that they would need about $20,000 in financing, so the two of them sat at Weinzweig's Smith Corona typewriter and typed out a business plan, which they intended to take to local banks to secure a loan. But in that bleak season, banks weren't readily lending. The nation and especially Michigan were mired in a recession that had cost the state tens of thousands of automobile industry jobs. The deli idea didn't seem like an attractive risk to area bankers, especially given the brief and unsuccessful track record of the previous tenant.

So, Saginaw decided to approach a property leasing company, seeing if he could get some value out of the equipment. It was a backdoor strategy, and sort of a Hail Mary pass. Before he secured the money, William McPherson III at the Huron Valley National Bank phoned back. He offered Saginaw $20,000 at 2 percent over the prime lending rate, then 20 percent, meaning the loan carried a 22 percent interest rate. Weinzweig subsequently borrowed some money from his grandmother to go with the loan, "and we were in business," Saginaw says.

They quickly cleaned the storefront and collected an initial group of suppliers, including their most important and most enduring: meat man Sy Ginsberg. Saginaw found Ginsberg through a mutual friend, Bennett Terebelo, a commercial real estate broker in the Detroit suburbs. Ginsberg had worked in delis since he was fifteen years old, dropping out of college so he could focus on his food career. For a time, he owned a place, and then branched into meat processing. When Saginaw called, Ginsberg had developed a sideline in advising deli owners, something he still does across the country. "I met them on Detroit Street in Ann Arbor one day and looked at the place," Ginsberg recalls. "They said, 'What do you think?'" Accustomed to suburban strip malls, he replied, "You're going to open up a deli here? Where's the parking lot? This location seems obscure." But Weinzweig and Saginaw impressed him with their enthusiasm. "They had the confidence," Ginsberg says, "so I said, 'I'm with you a hundred percent.'"

With almost lightning speed, Zingerman's Delicatessen opened on March 15, 1982.

WHO IS ZINGERMAN?

The Deli's name remains a subject of great curiosity among Zingerman's customers: Who, they ask, was Zingerman? Saginaw and Weinzweig admit being amused when someone comes into the Deli or the Roadhouse claiming to know the original Mr. Zingerman and demanding special treatment. The answer is that there was never a Mr. Zingerman, nor was there anyone with a Z in their last name who might have been the inspiration, like the Jewish custom of giving a baby a name that starts with the first letter of an honored forebearer. The men kicked around ideas that might have included their own names, but Weinzweig figured nobody would be able to pronounce his, and Saginaw's name could get mistaken for the Michigan city two hours north.

They settled on Greenberg's, which sounded appropriately Jewish. But a week before the deli was set to open, they discovered that the name was already taken by another business in Lansing. So, they scoured a phone book, but rather than start with an *A* at the top of the alphabet, they decided to choose a name starting with *Z*, at the end, thinking that it would stand out. (Greenberg lived on in the name of their first sandwich, "Who's Greenberg, Anyway," which has corned beef and chopped liver with Russian dressing on rye bread.)

Although Saginaw had managed restaurants, and Weinzweig had high aspirations for the food he wanted to sell, they quickly learned what they didn't know about running a business. "We were like little kids who got an electric guitar," Saginaw says. "We were really into music, we knew Clapton was great, Hendrix was great, but we didn't know how to play. Our ideas, our vision of what we wanted, exceeded our ability." Monahan says that's too modest. Saginaw and Weinzweig "had an idea of what they wanted to do, and they wanted to do the best," he says.

In retrospect, Saginaw says that their lack of experience was an advantage that they couldn't have gained if they had actually studied business in school. "I would never put down anybody who has a business degree," he says carefully, especially since several of Zingerman's managing partners have MBAs. "But we wanted to have fun. We didn't want to do anything in the normal way. We wanted to take an ordinary sandwich and make it extraordinary. After all, who goes out and borrows money at twenty-two percent to start a restaurant?"

Luckily for them, Ginsberg was there to help. Saginaw jokes that Ginsberg made the first sandwich ever served at the Deli, and Ginsberg admits it's probably true. "I'd deliver to them in the morning, and I'd stay and run the sandwich board until about noon," he says, "and then I'd train the help to make the sandwiches."

BALANCING EACH OTHER

Early on, Saginaw says their different approaches became apparent, and that was an advantage—one of the aspects that he thinks other entrepreneurs can emulate. "I naturally have a very, very high tolerance for risk. I am comfortable with a certain amount of chaos," he says. "Ari doesn't have a high tolerance for risk, but he has confidence in what he believes in. I don't need any data to make a decision; for Ari, there's never enough. We end up meeting in the middle." Saginaw realizes his willingness to gamble could be dangerous. "To this day, I think my level of confidence far exceeds my level of competence." But, he says, "I had Ari there. We've always been able to work things out."

Back in college, Weinzweig embraced the idea of being an anarchist—it is part of his personal brand (even though he disdains the very idea of personal brands). This requires an explanation. If you said "anarchist" to most people, they'd think of bomb throwers or violent protesters. In other words, anarchy equals chaos and something to fear.

But to Weinzweig, anarchy is "actually about a positive belief in human dignity and creativity, and the belief that every individual matters, and the disbelief in the value of hierarchy, which I think is unnatural," he said in an interview with *Vice*. Under old business models, there was a belief that business had to destroy the competition and grab the market for themselves. But by embracing a generosity of spirit, "you have the belief that the more you share, the better it goes for everyone."

He's since written a multipart series of books, *Zingerman's Guide to Good Leading: A Lapsed Anarchist's Approach* with individual topics such as building a great business, being a better leader, personal management, and beliefs in business. More titles in that series are in the works from Zingerman's Press, if you want to explore those subjects in depth. While he now calls himself a "lapsed anarchist," Weinzweig admits he's become less lapsed, and more enthusiastic about encouraging creativity and individualism.

Where Weinzweig describes himself as an introvert, Saginaw seems born to make deals. His wide smile, love of hats (he's worn fedoras before, during, and after they were cool with the hipster crowd), and background as a restaurant manager made him the perfect liaison to lenders and contractors. Put the pair together, says Ginsberg, and you have leaders that people want to work for. "Paul and Ari are two of the nicest people you could ever want to see. Ari's on the straight side, but Paul is a ton of fun," he says.

A CONSISTENT LOOK

From the beginning, Weinzweig and Saginaw wanted the Deli to feel cozy and memorable, even though minimalism was sweeping through the architecture, housewares, gourmet food, and restaurant worlds. Ann Arbor was a Midwest hub of Mid-century Modern design, thanks to noted architects like David Osler and Gunnar Birkerts. Chicago boasted Crate & Barrel, launched in 1962, bringing European simplicity and practicality to American shoppers. In England, Terence Conran founded his Habitat shops in 1964, aiming to replace chintz and overstuffed sofas with a sleeker look. In 1977, Joel Dean, Giorgio DeLuca, and Jack Ceglic opened their first Dean & DeLuca store, with an ultrasimple black-on-cream logo and labels.

Weinzweig says that elegant approach wasn't what he and Saginaw wanted. "I liked them, and they did great work, but I did not want to be like Dean & DeLuca," he says. "We definitely wanted to be way more accessible, way more down-to-earth, and that's been embedded since day one, in the writing and the messages." Rather than modernistic, Zingerman's logo became a sweeping signature headed up by an oversized Z, bringing to mind Zorro's famous slash. It looks like somebody's natural handwriting, half-printed, and half-cursive. In fact, it was a joint creation by Lori Saginaw and Steve Wallag-Muno, the Deli's fifteenth employee. Lori sketched the letters while Steve lengthened the tail of the Z so it underlined *Zingerman's*. He also made the letters look a little sharper than Saginaw's own writing did. "It's individual, it's colorful, it's bold, it's graphic, not corporate," says Wallag-Muno of the logo, which you can see on the cover of this book.

Along with the distinctive Zingerman's typeface—named Muno in his honor—Wallag-Muno initiated Zingerman's emphasis on graphic arts rather than photographs. If you receive a box from Zingerman's Mail Order, or simply look around the walls of many of its businesses, you'll see a variety of colorful cartoonlike characters and what appears to be freehand type. A fine-arts graduate from Michigan State University, Wallag-Muno loved the bold comic-book-style art that permeated the rock-and-roll scene in the 1960s and 1970s, featured in magazines like *Creem* and the work of cartoonist R. Crumb. While the Deli was often slammed with business at lunchtime, he had time to draw in the afternoons.

Wallag-Muno applied graphics to every part of the Deli. He sketched signs advertising new meats and cheeses, pictures of sandwiches, the faces of the owners, and regularly added new sandwich titles to the menu board, which Monahan had created. "They were open to it," Wallag-Muno says. "There's an individuality that we're selling. It comes from the heart." At one point, a goat cheese arrived from a Michigan farmer, and Wallag-Muno set out to illustrate it. "I tried drawing a goat, and it didn't turn out very well. He kind of looked like Pokey," the rubbery claymation pony from the television series. "So, I made up this goofy handwriting style," he says. "It felt fresh, it looked homemade, it felt different than the type I was buying. I was kind of a punk rock fan, and it had an edge to it. We started using it, more and more."

Wallag-Muno's approach remains Zingerman's signature look. He received a small piece of the business and stayed for ten years before heading to other jobs at the University of Michigan, with Borders Books & Music, and at his own firm, while remaining a Friend of Zingerman's, as those associated with the business are known. The graphic-arts responsibility was handed off to Ian Nagy, whom he had trained, and the company's team of graphic artists.

In its forty years, Zingerman's has never done a major redesign of its logo, nor has it changed its original whimsical feel, although there are rules now for how it's deployed. "We have written down what our look and feel is, and there are still arguments over how it's applied," Weinzweig says. Zingerman's graphic artists sometimes "get bored with the bold," he says, "but if the customer likes it, fine. And if you change it, what do you really achieve?" Wallag-Muno gleefully points out the spots where his original artwork remains (look for fading turquoise letters if you ever visit Zingerman's Next Door), and he keeps an archive of his work in his basement, including the original Zingerman's Mail Order catalog.

GREAT FOOD, GREAT SERVICE, GREAT TIMING

Timing is everything in business, and for Zingerman's, the timing could not have been better. Nationally, America was moving away from the obsession with frozen and processed food that had dominated the 1950s and 1960s, and the focus on vivid concoctions that marked the 1970s. By 1982, Chez Panisse, Alice Waters's groundbreaking restaurant in Berkeley, California, was a decade old, and the farm-to-table movement that she launched was beginning to be talked about around the country. Although the Food Network was still a decade away, some chefs had gained celebrity status, thanks to programs on commercial television as well as PBS.

In places like New York, Chicago, and San Francisco, dining out was the equivalent of an evening's entertainment. "Food is now the stuff of status," wine and restaurant critic Robert Finigan wrote in 1983. Diners were willing to experiment beyond takeout Chinese and try other international cuisines, such as sushi and Thai cuisine. They were sampling exotic produce like radicchio and jicama, products like sun-dried tomatoes, as well as goat cheese and different styles of yogurt besides Dannon's fruit-at-the-bottom kind. Ann Arbor, with its ever-changing population of academics and students from around the world, was a perfect laboratory.

Still, the early years were hard, and the Deli was far from an overnight success. Everybody involved in the venture pitched in, from employees to family members, and even vendors. Ginsberg made three trips a week to Ann Arbor, bringing meat that he loaded into the back of his Volkswagen—and the occasional sack of rye bread, too. Saginaw remembers a typical day had him up before dawn, going to Weinzweig's house to wake him up so he could open the Deli, and then driving into suburban Detroit to get bread. He was operating on only a few hours of sleep each night, because the Saginaws had their first child a year after the Deli opened. Some nights, he says he was so tired when he got home that he'd simply fall asleep on the couch, because he didn't have the energy to climb the stairs to the bedroom.

Even as Zingerman's was building its reputation, Saginaw was frustrated that it wasn't pulling more people in the door. In a typical summer, Ann Arbor bustles with 250,000 visitors to its annual Art Fair, spread across downtown. But, "during Art Fair, we were dead," Saginaw recalls. "Nobody knew about us." And while there was another 100,000 people who poured into Ann Arbor on football Saturdays and who would eventually provide a flood of business, they didn't find the Deli in the years right after it opened. "Only locals came out during the games," he says.

Saginaw theorizes that the Deli's small size might have given visitors the impression that little lay inside. Originally, it had just five tables and four stools in the front window—hard to believe, now that it covers four buildings and has a sprawling plaza for outdoor seating. But while it was still little-known even to locals, Zingerman's was becoming known within the gastronomic world as a place to watch as the artisan food movement was growing in the mid-1980s. Weinzweig's travels to food conferences, his trips to meet artisanal food producers, and the growing network he built among chefs, writers, and purveyors were paying off. By the time author and culinary teacher Molly Stevens met him in 1986, "He was already someone to pay attention to," she recalls. Now the crowds began to arrive, and the phenomenon known as "The Line" had begun.

PART TWO

Food and Philosophy

Since the beginning, Zingerman's has been known for whimsical illustrations. (Ian Nagy/Copyright 2021 DSE Inc.)

CHAPTER THREE

A Tour of Zingerman's Deli

A black-and-white awning at 422 Detroit Street reads *Zingerman's Deli-catessen*, below the same words embedded in the store's facade. On one side of the big wooden door sits a park bench, famous in Zingerman's history as the place where Weinzweig and Saginaw sat in 1992 to map out Zingerman's future (you'll read more about that in the next chapter). On the other side, there's a little ramp that complies with federal accessibility guidelines. If you're very lucky, you'll walk right into the Deli, as long as there's space inside. If you wind up waiting, you'll likely see people posing for pictures in front of the Deli, comparing notes about their favorite products, or chatting about their past Zingerman's experiences.

The wait is part of the experience, and real Zingerman's fans don't seem to mind the Line, as the horde of customers is known. "They've made Ann Arbor such a food mecca," says Alon Shaya, the chef and James Beard Award–winning restaurateur.

The Deli represents Weinzweig's belief that once people are exposed to good food, they will appreciate it, and find inherent value in it. Traditionally, many grocers believed "the standard flavorful foods should be reserved for an elusive upper-crust gourmet elite," he wrote in the *Zingerman's Guide to Good Eating*, published in 2003. "But the way I see it, good food is for everyone. I'm firm in my conviction that you don't have to have been born French or be an insufferable food snob to discern the difference between a well-made farmhouse cheese and a bland, rubbery factory version that bears the same name."

He went on, "Armed with a little background information, a heightened sense of awareness, and a shopping bag filled with great ingredients, almost anyone who's interested can understand, prepare, and appreciate top-quality food." Accompanying that belief is a warm welcome to the center of Zingerman's universe, the Deli. No matter the time of day, or the number of people waiting, someone will greet you when you arrive, whether it's the staff member stationed at the door, the employee behind the bread counter, or a person helping another customer find what they're seeking.

As you enter, you see Zingerman's black-and-white tile floor, the kind found in so many fish and meat markets and grocery stores from the 1800s until today. To the right of the door, you'll see shelves holding dozens of books. Many are written by Weinzweig, including titles detailing the company's history, its food, and its management principles. There are also cookbooks, including the one for Zingerman's Bakehouse, and others by authors who have appeared at its events or taught classes, who are known as Friends of Zingerman's. Next to the books is a coffee grinder and shelves holding different blends from Zingerman's Coffee Company, which you can purchase as whole beans or have ground to the texture you need for your French press, Chemex, or plain old coffeemaker.

To the left of the door, you'll find a small refrigerator case with bright pink smoked salmon fillets, ready to be sliced, and containers of spreadable cheeses from Zingerman's Creamery. These include cream cheese, which was its first cheese product (specifically made for Zingerman's bagels), goat cheese, and a packaged version of the pimiento cheese that's a popular appetizer at Zingerman's Roadhouse, its sit-down restaurant on the west side of Ann Arbor that specializes in classic American food.

Across the aisle, you'll find the "bread box," an enclosed sales area where products like bread loaves from Zingerman's Bakehouse fill shelves up to the ceiling. Coffee cakes wrapped in transparent film are within easy reach. There are tall dowels of bagels—the thin, chewy kind that date back to the early 1900s, not the fat, puffy ones that are more like bread rolls—in flavors like traditional, sesame, poppy seed, and roasted garlic. Next to them is a tray of pastries, such as cinnamon rolls, muffins, and croissants stuffed with prosciutto and Parmesan.

PROVISIONS TO PUT BETWEEN THE BREAD

If you're there for meats and cheeses, you simply have to turn to the other side of the store, where cases filled with choices await. When I studied cooking in Paris, Patricia Wells took us to a small shop in the Seventh Arrondissement called Marie Quatrehomme. It was the first place I saw burrata, the elastic mozzarella filled with thick cream, and the tiny shop overflowed with other cheeses from across France and around the world. Zingerman's cheese section is like that *fromagerie*. About fifty varieties are in plain view, spread across two refrigerator cases, but there can be easily twice that many on shelves behind the cheese mongers and stored in the back.

On one visit, I watched a Zingerman's staffer accompany a customer to the cheese case. The gentleman had picked out a loaf of Zingerman's bread and was interested in a cheese to serve with it. The staffer zeroed in on Saint Angel, listed at twenty-eight dollars a pound, and began telling him about its qualities. A hand-lettered tag described it as a cow's milk cheese that was "a beautiful, mushroomy, mild triple cream that melts in your mouth." The customer looked satisfied, and the sale was made. If he had wanted something else, the case also held entire wheels of blue cheeses, like Bleu des Basques, a sheep's milk cheese from France; Faribault blue, a cow's milk cheese from Minnesota; and French Bleu d'Auvergne. Name any kind of handcrafted cheese, from massive wheels of Parmesan to spreadable rounds of chèvre, and Zingerman's is likely to have it.

The long row of cheeses merges into dozens of cured meats, from whole smoked sausages (encased in plastic so that their aroma does not interfere with the cheeses) as well as an extensive selection of bacon. A prime spot is given to Nueske's, the Wisconsin company that has been in business since the Great Depression. The Deli was one of its earliest customers as it built its national wholesale business. You'll find full slabs of Nueske's signature applewood smoked bacon, and another of a more recent product, cherrywood smoked bacon. While both are sold prepackaged in supermarkets, a Zingerman's staffer behind the counter stands ready to slice slabs to order. You can take home as few slices as you want, and request the thickness you wish.

After you ponder your way through pepperoni, bologna and salami, Iberian and American hams, gaze at truffle mousse and chorizo, there's yet another case in a corner. This one holds big jars of Zingerman's own snappy pickles, in new (garlic, fresh dill, and vinegar) and old (a stronger garlic flavor) varieties, the same ones that come with its Deli sandwiches. You'll find house-made ranch and Russian dressings, and some small containers of popular salads like coleslaw, sesame noodles, and potato salad. Not far away stands a freezer, this one about six feet tall, with prepackaged piecrusts, containers of gelato and frozen babka, ready to come home with you.

BUILDING THE DELI

When Weinzweig and Saginaw drafted their typewritten business plan forty years ago, big-city delis were vanishing, as their Jewish customers moved to the suburbs. The traditional abundance that delis represented, with their meaty sandwiches, chopped liver, rich salads, potato pancakes, knishes, and big pickles, was falling out of favor. "In many cities, delis no longer exist," wrote David Sax in his book *Save the Deli*. "Traditional products are disappearing from menus and shelves because they don't fit into the bottom line. As have gone the Jews, so, too, have gone their nearby delis."

But nostalgia was a strong motivator for people who enjoyed deli food and could no longer find it, and there were new generations to whom these vintage tastes could be introduced, especially if the dishes were better than their parents and grandparents had eaten. The goal for Saginaw and Weinzweig wasn't just to open a deli. It was to open an *outstanding* deli. "If I give you a taste of something, it is likely it is going to be the best whatever I just gave you that you tasted in your life," says Deli managing partner Rick Strutz. "Even if they don't buy, they have that memory of what it tasted like."

Ginsberg, the meat man, sees a difference between what delis were to prior generations and what they later became. "The old version, you got sliced meats and salad and pickles, and there was lots of fish and cheese. Now people are calling glorified sandwich shops delis, too. They're borrowing the fact that if it's corned beef and pastrami and turkey, we can call it a deli." At the outset, Ginsberg didn't know if Saginaw and Weinzweig had the right instincts, since they weren't raised in family businesses the way so many deli owners were. Weinzweig admits that while his grandmother was a great cook, and he ate at Jewish delis, his family food heritage was lacking. "I grew up on Kraft macaroni and cheese, fish sticks, and Cheetos," he says. "No one was in the business, they were teachers, doctors, and lawyers. I was sort of the failure of the family," for getting his history degree and working in restaurants.

Says Ginsberg, "I was concerned at first, until I realized how bright they were, and how easily they could figure things out. It takes some degree of intelligence." Once he jumped on board helping out, the cooking lessons began. Ginsberg started by teaching them how to prepare his corned beef, which begins as brisket. "You get the corned beef raw, and you cook it. A lot of people will, in my opinion, undercook it," he says of recipes that call for a two-hour simmer. "You get a better yield, but you have to shave it thin to make it decently edible. If it's on the thicker side, it's too chewy," he says. Ginsberg taught the Zingerman's owners to cook the brisket for three and a half to four hours. "It's not going to yield [as much], but it will deliver the most tender sandwich you can imagine. That's the one important thing I stress to them."

The bread had to be right, too. Ginsberg suggested that the Deli use double-baked, hand-sliced rye bread. That meant getting the loaves not quite fully baked, then putting them in an oven for fiteen to twenty minutes to create a crusty exterior and warm interior. "Then you slice it at an angle by hand—not on a slicer machine," he says. "That gives you the crunch on the crust and brings out the flavor of the bread. Those are the two most important things—corned beef and bread." But Ginsberg says Zingerman's was willing to take things a step further than even his high standards. He was startled to see Zingerman's use imported Swiss cheese, even though the owners could easily find a domestically made substitute. "I don't know anybody who uses imported Swiss cheese anymore," he says. "Put those all together, and it's what makes Zingerman's so good."

Artist Wallag-Muno says food education for Zingerman's staff started right at the beginning. "The minute I walked in, they thrust a three-ring binder at me, full of articles about prosciutto and olive oil" that he was expected to read. "I said, 'You mean you can get oil from olives?'" (Weinzweig admits the approach was somewhat aspirational. "When we opened, we had two olive oils. Most people had none," he says.) Saginaw says he realizes that Zingerman's insistence on stocking top-quality products at a time when they were just becoming familiar to consumers was risky from a financial point of view. "If you went to the business school back then and asked them, 'What's the market for goat cheese and aged vinegar?' they'd come back and say, 'Don't bother opening.'" By contrast, the Zingerman's partners believed, "Well, we love this, and we think other people will love it," Saginaw says.

When he first started doing business with the Deli, Ginsberg estimated that he sold Zingerman's about six hundred pounds of meat a week. Four decades later, that stood at four thousand to five thousand pounds weekly. Ginsberg says he still sometimes can't believe Zingerman's success. "It's so unfathomable to me, on a football Saturday in Ann Arbor, that anybody would wait in a line around the corner to get sandwiches to take to the ball game," he says. "You travel around the country, and Zingerman's is known all over the place. It's fun, a lot of fun to be able to say I'm part of them."

THE SPICE TRADE

The Deli is much more than bread, meat, and cheese. When you turn the corner next to the coffee and the books, your eyes are greeted by a floor-to-ceiling display of bottles, jars, tins, paper packages, and other containers bearing gourmet groceries. It takes a moment to absorb everything that's there, and you might feel flummoxed trying to figure it all out. But you won't be left alone for long. A Zingerman's staff member is standing nearby, able to offer detailed specifics on any of the products. While I was browsing, I overheard a customer asking about the merits of two different types of dried peppers. As the staff member in spices gave her a rundown, the employee behind the bread counter chimed in. Soon the customer knew not only the history of the peppers, but their origin, and different types of uses for each. I smiled because the pepper in question was supplied to Zingerman's by a company that I knew well: Épices de Cru, whose shop is in the Jean-Talon Market in Montreal.

Épices de Cru is a rabbit warren of a place, long and narrow, with floor-to-ceiling shelves on either side of the room. It is owned by Philippe and Ethné de Vienne—he a French Canadian chef, she from Trinidad—who decided to segue into the spice world after other careers. On my visits to Montreal, I regularly brought home their small aluminum tins of spices, decorated with simple cream labels and red lettering. The shop offered an enormous selection of vanilla beans, and products that were harder to find in the United States, such as kefir lime leaves and lemongrass.

One day, a customer ventured inside: Weinzweig, who took every opportunity he could during business trips to search for top-quality products. "Ari walked into the store, and said, 'Hey, you've got a lot of spices, where do I start?'" Ethné de Vienne recalls. Her daughter waited on him as de Vienne listened in. To her, Weinzweig looked as if he had found water in the desert. "He walked away and said, 'I don't believe what just happened,'" she says. Weinzweig says he didn't set out specifically to find the store. He wanted to escape from a dull session of the American Cheese Society conference, which was being held in Montreal, and decided to visit one of the city's food markets. He randomly picked Marché Jean-Talon from a list and was wandering its aisles of fresh produce and peeking into its little shops when he stumbled upon Épices de Cru.

"Spices were something I was interested in, but we hadn't gotten into" carrying them, he says. Weinzweig bought a few tins but says he couldn't see doing business directly with the de Viennes, because of complexities of importing their products from Canada. But a few months later, the de Viennes were at the Fancy Food Show in New York City, an annual event showcasing gourmet food from around the world. A change in trade laws had eliminated some of the red tape that complicated shipping to the United States, and the de Viennes were actively looking for American customers. Weinzweig, now familiar with the company's logo and the quality of its spices, spotted their booth down the aisle of the trade show and took the entire Zingerman's team over to meet them. That gave the de Viennes a feel for what working with Zingerman's would be like. "We vet people as much as we hope they would vet us," Ethné says.

Weinzweig says he was happy to find a trustworthy supplier whose owners had the same approach to researching new products as he did. "I wasn't ready to carve out a year and a half to devote" to studying spices, he says. In the initial order, Épices de Cru supplied Zingerman's about ten different types of spices; by 2022, it was up to more than one hundred, and the relationship became one of the most important for both companies.

Épices de Cru became the centerpiece of a Zingerman's event called Spice Week, with presentations at the Deli, classes on using spices, and a dinner at the Roadhouse. The company's curry mixture is used at the Deli on its turkey curry salad, the Roadhouse uses its Tellicherry pepper on french fries and other dishes, and Épices de Cru spices appear on the lineup of toast items offered at Zingerman's Coffee. Customers can buy a set of spices specially packaged for Zingerman's, and the Épices de Cru cookbook is also available for sale at the Deli. "It costs more," Weinzweig says of the spice company's lineup, "but everything we do costs more." While the de Viennes have had many offers to sell their products in big Canadian and American chain stores, "We're happy with little retailers who are happy with us," Ethné de Vienne says. "It's always been our growth strategy and it continues to be our strategy. We're interested in people who are interested in us."

VINEGAR AND OLIVE OIL

Today, balsamic vinegar is an obsession among many food lovers, attracting streams of visitors to Modena, Italy, where everything about authentic balsamic vinegar is regulated, down to the shape of the bottle and the seal on its stopper. When Zingerman's began carrying it, however, grocery-store vinegar essentially came in two flavors—white vinegar, which could be used as a cleaning agent as well as a salad dressing, and red wine vinegar. (The latter was still so unusual in the early 1980s that when my mother served it on her salads, friends would ask her to bring the bottle out to show them.) There were only a few flavored vinegars available in specialty stores. My mother made her own, flavoring white vinegar with sprigs of dill or rosemary.

Balsamic vinegar's popularity in the United States is generally attributed to Chuck Williams, the founder of Williams Sonoma, who began selling it in his gourmet stores in 1977. But the product has strict preparation and taste standards, as I learned in a class on balsamic vinegar that I took at Zingerman's. True balsamic is produced only in the Italian regions of Modena and Reggio Emilia. Production is overseen from start to finish by an official Italian certification agency, which also operates a tasting commission. The process begins with whole pressed grapes, including the juice, skin, seeds, and stems. Technically, a balsamic vinegar can be sold after fermenting for as little as ninety days, but the bare minimum that most gourmet stores sell is a year, and the vinegars sold by Zingerman's are much older than that.

Why does it matter? you might ask. Well, younger vinegars have a bright and tart taste, but as the vinegar ages, it becomes thicker and sweeter, with some of the oldest vinegars as thick and flavorful as honey. Many people don't realize that you aren't supposed to cook with balsamic vinegar, because heat will ruin the flavor. Even balsamic vinegar salad dressing is not a great use of it, because oil dampens down the fermented flavor. Instead, it's the ultimate drizzling vinegar—a true dressing, in that you "dress" berries, cheese, vegetables, or sweets like ice cream or flan with it, or put some drops on top of grilled chicken, fish, or meat.

This is all helpful to know when you face the wall of balsamic vinegars that Zingerman's sells. The first thing you might notice is a big pink-and-red arrow that points to a row of ten-year-old balsamic vinegar, in tall bottles with a Zingerman's label, priced at thirty-five dollars. *Our best everyday vinegar!* the arrow declares. (It is good; I've bought several bottles through the years.) Above it sits a selection of sixteen-year-old vinegar, in a shorter, stout bottle, at forty-five dollars. There's a thirty-dollar sampler kit, with four small bottles in a box, allowing you to taste different ages of balsamic. I received one of these in my tasting class, and it is fun to figure out which vinegar is right for which purpose.

Then there's an olive oil section, which Zingerman's teaches about, too. The growth of this section of the store reflects how Weinzweig learned more about the product. Even though he stocked quality olive oil from the beginning, it took him until the 1990s to attend his first olive oil harvest. He made a pilgrimage to Italy, visiting three producers, and learned about the "emotional intensity" that accompanies the process. Weinzweig discovered that there can be numerous differences that distinguish good olive oil, from the type of olives used to the age of the trees, the growing conditions, and the type of equipment used to press the oil, whether old-fashioned, hand-operated mills or more modern equipment.

Zingerman's customers can meet these producers in person, through the Food Tours that the company has conducted since 1997, or for local residents, in a class held every year called Ari's Favorite Things. In it, Weinzweig highlights the best products the Deli introduced that year—usually as many as thirty or thirty-five new ones, and invites selected makers to join him. (In 2020, it was held virtually, but the products featured in the class were readily available from the Deli or from Zingerman's Mail Order.)

Unless you have unlimited time to browse either the store or Mail Order's website, Ari's Favorite Things is a great way to learn about new products and keep up on food trends. It is traditionally held before the Christmas holidays, either upstairs in the Deli's sprawling seating area or at one of Zingerman's events spaces elsewhere in Ann Arbor. It's like the Mail Order catalog come to life. When they sit down, guests receive a list of around thirty to forty different products, and as Weinzweig talks, servers move through the group passing out samples to try—like small plates of the newest pasta on the shelves, cooked and tossed with olive oil or Parmesan, various cheeses from different parts of the world, small plastic cups of red walnuts and others bearing different sips of vinegar or olive oil. It's important to come hungry, because it's like the tasting menu of an upscale restaurant, only with retail products that you can purchase and take home.

A few years ago, my friend Luke Song, the milliner who designed Aretha Franklin's famous gray hat with a rhinestone bow for Barack Obama's inauguration, joined me at the class. We were enthralled by one producer, Marques de Valdueza, which has produced olive oil on its farm since 1624. We watched a slide show that explained that its olive harvesting is a carefully timed procedure that minimizes the time from picking to processing. The olive oil, with a distinctive baby-blue label, is priced at thirty-seven dollars. Of course, lots of gourmet stores sell such products, but in the case of the Deli, you are able to learn the heritage behind everything it sells—and, as with Marques de Valdueza and the de Viennes from Montreal, you might get to meet the person who makes it. Luke subsequently purchased the olive oil for Christmas gifts, and I continually refresh my supply.

On any visit to the Deli, or another Zingerman's business, you're likely to bump into one of the managing partners who are in charge of the place. During one casual trip, I spotted Grace Singleton, one of the Deli's three managing partners, chatting with a member of the staff. Singleton presided over one of the best presentations I've ever seen at Zingerman's, which told the story of Parmesan cheese and what goes into making it. The Deli's upstairs seating area was packed as Singleton showed off an enormous wheel of Parmigiano-Reggiano, which only 329 dairies in Italy are sanctioned to produce. Singleton has visited a number of them over the years, and even led Food Tours with Weinzweig.

On this evening, under her supervision, cheese staffers from the Deli carefully marked spots along the top and sides of the wheel where they inserted *grana* knives, which look like little flat garden trowels. As Singleton told us about the production process, we tasted different ages of the cheese, our eyes occasionally darting away to watch the progress being made in opening the wheel, so big it would cover the surface of a round, two-top bar table. I remember holding my breath when it was time to reveal its interior, hoping it wouldn't fall apart, a sign that it hadn't aged properly. The room broke into applause when the wheel split open to show the pale yellow, granulated pieces inside.

Singleton's Deli partner, Rick Strutz, says communication among employees is constant—about Zingerman's philosophy, techniques for selling, as well as information about the products themselves. Programs like the cheese class are just some of the ways that staff members, and even partners, learn. "There's no way you have the answer to everything, with that amount of product," Strutz says. "You are always going to need help. You are always going to have to ask somebody for something." For other managers, it might be embarrassing not to have an answer at their fingertips. But at Zingerman's, "It's great to ask for help, and to get it from everyone around you. It creates a real team atmosphere."

The Deli is such a fascinating place that you might wonder why there is only one. Surely, Zingerman's could have easily franchised, or at least duplicated, its operations. And, at one point, Zingerman's thought seriously about doing that. There were plans to put a version of Zingerman's Deli in the Detroit Metropolitan Airport, which opened a sparkling new terminal in spring 2001, but the project was canceled after the September 11 attacks. In retrospect, a second Deli would have run counter to the path Zingerman's had already decided to take, one that was set forth when Saginaw dragged Weinzweig out to the bench in front of the Deli in 1992 to begin a conversation about the company's future.

CHAPTER FOUR

Guiding Principles

Maybe the Deli didn't feel like an overnight success to the people most closely involved, but four years into its existence, it had gained a solid fan base of locals and added seven hundred square feet of much-needed space to the sandwich production line in its kitchen to respond to customer demand. Although that growth was an early sign of success, neither Weinzweig nor Saginaw can pick out one moment in those first years when they felt Zingerman's had made it. "We had our heads down, trying not to scream at each other," he jokes. Adds Weinzweig, "I didn't [know] then, and I definitely don't now. You're always improving, and you're always failing."

Even as the business grew, the cofounders were determined to give back. A few days before Thanksgiving 1988, Zingerman's launched Food Gatherers, a charity aimed at alleviating food waste across the community and feeding those in need. A handful of volunteers commandeered a van and visited half a dozen grocery stores and restaurants, picking up 50 pounds of eggs, milk, and bread, and taking them to hot meal programs in Ann Arbor and Ypsilanti. (More than thirty years later, it has grown to 7,500 volunteers, who have handled 6.6 million pounds of food since its inception.) Along with serving the community, Zingerman's was meeting its goal of being a place where customers wanted to shop and employees liked to work.

"People were smiling and we were able to get the early staff really excited about our food," Saginaw says.

As the business developed, Saginaw and Weinzweig continually discussed ways to grow and improve, fueled by ideas gleaned from books they traded back and forth. Every year, they'd agree on a goal for the Deli, things like, "Let's improve the turkey," Saginaw recalls. His drive to keep improving came out of his admiration for W. Edwards Deming, the American quality expert who visited postwar Japan in 1950 to assist Toyota and a variety of companies with rebuilding themselves and finding new markets. Famous in Japan, where he was honored by Emperor Hirohito, he was little known at home. In 1980, NBC aired the documentary *If Japan Can . . . Why Can't We?* and Deming's work launched a widespread interest in quality, fueled by rising sales of cars from the Japanese companies he had helped rebuild.

During the Deli's early days, Saginaw encountered Deming's 14 Points for Management, which stress consistency of purpose, emphasize job training, encourage leaders to drive out fear so staff can work without worry, and involve everyone in the enterprise. (See the Appendix for Deming's famous 14 Points for Total Quality Management, concepts Saginaw embraced with enthusiasm.) At that point, the Deli wasn't making much beyond sandwiches and salads, but Saginaw knew that if it ever wanted to do more, Zingerman's would need a clearly defined culture. Deming was known for saying, "The customer didn't invent the lightbulb," in contrast with the widely held belief that customers were always right. (Or as Henry Ford put it, "If I had asked people what they wanted, they would have said a faster horse.") In Deming's view, this was a key leadership principle. While customer feedback is important, and input should always be welcomed, it's up to leaders to set a company's direction.

In 1992, a decade after the Deli was founded and had initially expanded, Saginaw was itching to grow further. At that point, the Deli was generating about $6 million a year in annual sales, winning praise from national publications, and attracting customers who would happily wait in line for an opportunity to order sandwiches and take home meats and cheeses. Although it didn't yet have a formal Mail Order business, it occasionally got phone orders for groceries from out of town, which a Deli staffer would pack up and drop off at a local post office.

For Weinzweig, the Deli represented exactly what he hoped to get out of the venture. The food was delicious, customers were satisfied, and he had plenty of time to research the items he wanted to sell, travel in search of interesting products, read up on food history, and work on the books he hoped to eventually publish. A milestone for him came in 1990 when he made his first research trip to investigate the cheese-making industry in Ireland, which was beginning its economic renaissance. He met some of Ireland's best-known culinary figures, such as Myrtle Allen, owner of The Yeats Room restaurant at the famed Ballymaloe House and cooking school, and the Ferguson family, known for their farmhouse cheeses. Weinzweig's explorations illustrated a landmark Toyota principle, *genchi genbutsu*, which translates as "go and see," or "go to the spot," and it fit perfectly with the philosophy he wanted Zingerman's to embrace. "Until you go to a cheese shop in Greece, you don't know that there are nine kinds of feta," he says. That drive to explore led him to countries such as Croatia and Tunisia, cities like San Francisco and New Orleans, and states across the American South, helping him make more Friends of Zingerman's along the way.

While Saginaw was pleased by the Deli's accomplishments and happy to let Weinzweig go exploring for new products, he saw the situation facing Zingerman's through a different lens. As the partner in charge of overseeing the financial operations, he was beginning to get offers from investors who wanted to replicate the Deli in other towns. Even without Zingerman's permission, the Deli's practices were being copied. That led to a lengthy legal dispute that changed Zingerman's direction for good. Even now, you can hear the pain in Saginaw's voice when he talks about it.

The showdown between Zingerman's and Amer's Mediterranean Deli focused on one of the basic tenets of the restaurant business: There are no patents on restaurant recipes. While there are some legal protections for creative ventures, "It's not like the police are going to come," Saginaw says. Even at the highest levels of the industry, chefs freely admit to being inspired by each other's ideas. "I'm always looking at what colleagues are doing," says Vishwesh Bhatt, the James Beard Award–winning chef at Snackbar in Oxford, Mississippi. "I try something, and say, 'We can do that.' Blatantly stealing from someone is one way" to introduce new dishes, he says.

Amer's began as a single Ann Arbor deli, then it opened a second one on State Street, facing Michigan's central campus, about a fifteen-minute walk from Zingerman's. The Zingerman's Deli was clearly an inspiration for Amer's design. It had a similar checkered tile floor and a colorful menu board, listing the numbers and names of its sandwiches, plus a newsletter similar to Zingerman's, with quirky artwork. It seemed so much like Zingerman's that some customers thought it *was* Zingerman's, Saginaw maintains. "We realized the customers were confused. We'd get a phone call, and they'd complain about their order. As you questioned it, they didn't buy it from us, they bought it from Amer's," Saginaw says.

Weinzweig and Saginaw say they tried asking politely for Amer's to cease and desist. "You'd make a phone call, send a fax over. No response, no response, no response," Saginaw says. In 1993, Zingerman's decided to take Amer's to court, accusing them of "trade dress"—copying its style and its atmosphere. In response, Amer's vehemently denied it was copying Zingerman's, saying that its features were similar to those in delis everywhere. It responded that the lawsuit was simply about money and that Zingerman's was simply afraid of competition. The legal dispute dragged on another fourteen years, until a settlement in 2007. Amer's remains in business on State Street, selling coffee, tea, sandwiches, and salads.

Before finally taking legal action, Saginaw did some soul-searching. He realized some of the situation was Zingerman's own fault. "People aren't stupid. They can see the line out the door, they can see what's profitable and doesn't sell. They can open up a few blocks from you, they can offer thirty percent of the quality for sixty percent of the price," he says. "We got smug, and arrogant, and looked like we owned the market, and nobody was going to take it from us."

Saginaw decided that "we can't comfortably sit here and have this little cute deli and think life is going to go on and be ideal." The only way for Zingerman's to protect itself, he decided, was by improving what it was doing, extending its product lines, and layering innovation on top of that. It was time, Saginaw thought, for Zingerman's to think seriously about becoming a bigger company, and the greater potential it could offer its owners, employees, and the larger community beyond a single deli and the charitable work it did through Food Gatherers. Along with the potential lines of business that Zingerman's could set up, the questions in his mind included, "How are we going to behave in the world? What is our orientation toward racial justice, social justice, environmental justice? Do we continue to offer opportunities? Can we increase wages? How are we going to do it?" Saginaw says.

One stumbling block to expansion, however, was that Zingerman's had tried, and spectacularly failed, to operate a produce business during the 1980s in the Kerrytown Market Building, where Monahan's fish business was located. The Zingerman's partners found that they lacked the skills, time, and vendors to maintain a business selling fresh fruits and vegetables, and Zingerman's Produce is only remembered now by a few locals like me who shopped there. The failure, in contrast to the Deli's success, made Weinzweig gun-shy about expanding beyond Detroit Street. Once they began talking about a bigger future, Weinzweig was eventually convinced to go along with Saginaw's push to create a broader enterprise, mainly because he saw the good it could do for Zingerman's employees and the community. However, he dug his heels in on a crucial point: He wanted to keep everything in Ann Arbor.

The decision to remain in one location "makes everything easier. The more you act like you're going to be there, the more you want to be there, and the more difference you can make," Saginaw says.

Beyond that, Weinzweig "wanted to create a special place, where people would be driven to go a long way to come to," he says. "I was like, 'I want to have one, and make it really cool and special. I just have never liked it when I went into unit five,'" he says of establishments with multiple outlets. "Everything would be present, but the vibrancy, the authenticity, the vibe are all missing." He also worried that what made Zingerman's special could not be reproduced by outsiders who weren't there for its founding, or who did not understand its approach to business, and that Zingerman's own approach could become diluted by the carbon copies. To him, the most important thing simply could not change: the devotion to food.

THE CONCEPT OF VISIONING

In a Hollywood movie, Weinzweig and Saginaw would have concluded their initial 1992 conversation about the future of Zingerman's by shaking hands and getting to work. In reality, a concrete plan took about two years to come to fruition as the pair debated what Zingerman's should be. The lengthy discussions became a Zingerman's hallmark, and until the pandemic, movement on even small decisions could take months or years. Saginaw says he was completely aware that growth would be difficult, especially since neither he nor Weinzweig had formal business training or any experience in expanding a business. Remembering the difficulties that Monahan had had with his fish business, Saginaw dove into business books for help, starting with *The Empowered Manager* by Peter Block and *The End of Bureaucracy and the Rise of the Intelligent Organization* by Gifford and Elizabeth Pinchot. These books offered practical advice aimed at helping managers avoid creating too much bureaucracy and nurturing an entrepreneurial spirit, and encouraged leaders to tap into the skills of every employee, not just managers. "It struck me that we had a mission"— which was to grow—"but not a vision," Saginaw says.

That lengthy discussion marked the first instance in which Zingerman's used the process called Visioning, which has become a part of every significant step it has taken ever since. Simply put, Visioning means drafting a description of success for a point in the future. A vision isn't a mission statement, and it doesn't include the steps to get there. Those are filled in as things go along.

The process was difficult, Saginaw says. "It was like pulling teeth to get him to understand the whole concept," he says of Weinzweig. "How are you going to say you are going to do something, but you aren't able to do it [now]?" But Weinzweig ultimately became a convert, and then an evangelist for the idea. He regularly teaches a class in Visioning at Zing-Train, the Zingerman's training organization that was set up in 1994. Visioning can be both inspiring and uncomfortable. It departs from the traditional "set a goal, then achieve it" mentality that has been common in the corporate world, and even at small businesses as well. "A vision is the actual destination," Weinzweig writes. "It's a vivid description of what 'success' looks and feels like for us—what we are able to achieve, and the effect that it has on our staff."

There are four things that go into an effective vision. First, it needs to be **inspiring**—something that an individual, or part of the organization truly wants to achieve. Second, it needs to be **strategically sound**. There's no point in drafting a vision that will bankrupt the company, or which costs so much time, money, and effort that it causes damage. Third, the vision has to be **written down**. Simply kicking around ideas is not a vision. Fourth, the vision needs to be **communicated**. It can't be a document that you print out and then put in a desk drawer. In order for it to be effective, those who wrote the vision have to share it with others.

Weinzweig says visions can be applied to ideas, to entire organizations, and used for personal growth, too. You can write a vision for a wedding, a restaurant, a shop, a product line. The whole idea is to leapfrog from today to the future that could be. You're writing what is in essence a screenplay for the story that your company will tell X years hence. I've included Zingerman's lengthy vision for 2032 at the end of the book, but here's a shorter one, written by Weinzweig, for a smaller venture—the farmer's market that Zingerman's has operated in the parking lot of Zingerman's Roadhouse for about a dozen years.

A THURSDAY EVENING FARMER'S MARKET IN THE PARKING LOT OF ZINGERMAN'S ROADHOUSE—THE VISION (WRITTEN IN 2005)

Throngs of people are milling around the Roadhouse parking lot on this Thursday, amazed and excited at the abundance of locally produced goods and services ranging from several varieties of tomatoes to handmade soap and artisan crafts, to herbs and plants, plus Zingerman's items—cheese from the Creamery, breads from the Bakehouse, and the ever-energetic Roadshow crew caffeinating all the vendors and customers. Every vendor is selling the best of what they are growing or producing. There's a tangible truth patrons have come to trust—that all these products have a story and none of them traveled far to get here. Tents and awnings cover the stalls, creating a colorful and festive mood. There are fifteen to twenty vendors at the West Side Farmer's Market, so it's accessible and maintains variety but remains magnetic and welcoming.

The Market continues to provide customers with the best products available and serves as a catalyst for community development by offering an educational component and a local music scene. We have space reserved for weekly acts, including local musicians, demonstrations, and other activities. Several people recognize the Roadhouse chefs selecting vegetables from the Market's vendors for their weekend's menus. The Market is a family event, where parents bring their children to shop for fresh produce and enjoy a snack at our picnic tables. Guests are thrilled with the produce, the chance to visit with neighbors, and best of all, connect with the farmers who actually grow their food.

This year, the planning committee is generating support throughout the business community. Local businesses hang posters about the Market and participate in promotions. These companies recognize the potential for the Market to draw additional patrons to the area, enabling the Market to become a more self-sustaining entity. The Market planning committee operates under an inspiring mission statement and is taking steps toward making it a fiscally independent operation. The Market manager is working closely with the Zingerman's liaison to ensure organization and success, from honing job descriptions to developing and proposing paid Market positions. We have a great group of vendors working together who are already excited to build on these successes for next year. Visions and action steps are laid out for the coming years at our annual Market debrief.

Visioning, Weinzweig says, is a way to keep people focused on the ultimate big picture, or to keep their eyes on the prize. "Because while most of our day-to-day work may be mundane, the vision is special—it's a picture of the beautiful 'cathedral' that we're all working together to build. And it helps keep us excited to overcome the inevitable challenges that come up." He and Saginaw used this process to write Zingerman's original vision, which painted a picture of how the company would look in 2009. You can read more about the result in Chapter 6, but the pair agreed that Zingerman's would become a collective of companies, and that every business they started needed to be run by someone who was as passionate as they were about food, service, and financial results. "There were so many things we wanted to do," Saginaw remembers.

OPEN BOOK MANAGEMENT

As a business journalist, I always try to get as much financial data as possible from the companies I write about. That's relatively easy to do with publicly held companies, like the big automakers or airlines or retailers. If they sell stock, they are required by the Securities and Exchange Commission to publish quarterly results, with profit and loss statements, and balance sheets. Some sectors of industry release monthly snapshots, or even more frequent updates. When I began writing about the automakers in the late-twentieth century, companies even released ten-day car sales numbers.

But privately held companies, and especially family-owned companies, keep much of their financial information to themselves. If they aren't willing to discuss their revenues and profits, journalists and others must find ways to get information. Sometimes, it's available when companies ask for tax abatements from local communities. It might be found in reports to the federal government, such as when a business changes ownership, buys property, or acquires another business. And it will turn up if the organization tells the state that they will be making permanent layoffs or closing down.

Zingerman's is an incredible exception to that veil of secrecy, so much so that I sometimes couldn't believe the amount of information that the company's chief administrative officer, Ron Maurer, and the managing partners were willing to share for this book. The reason is their philosophy of Open Book Management. It allows anyone at any level of the company, whether managing partner or employee, to see applicable numbers. But, because not everyone can absorb the meaning of a balance sheet without a financial background, Zingerman's also gives them an education and tools to understand what they are seeing, and how those numbers can fluctuate depending on the conditions that affect the business.

As Zingerman's puts it, Open Book Management tells the story behind the numbers on a scoreboard. "It's a little harder sometimes" to share the information, says Singleton, a managing partner at the Deli, "but there's also a lot of strength in it."

Open Book Management came into being at Zingerman's in 2002—twenty years after the Deli was founded, as the group of businesses that Weinzweig and Saginaw envisioned was coming to life. In the course of his constant research, Weinzweig got the idea from SRC Holdings Company, which remanufactures products for a variety of industries, such as agricultural, industrial, construction, truck, marine, and automotive (its machinery is typically 30 to 60 percent cheaper than buying new). With Zingerman's now growing at a rapid pace, and with different parts of its organization dependent on the others for success, it made sense to share the numbers across the businesses so that employees could get a multidimensional view.

But it was a pretty radical idea, and it required some structure. So, Zingerman's businesses came up with a way to share information. On a regular basis, every business holds a huddle, a meeting where metrics are reported and explained. The goal is to understand what the numbers mean, how they measure up to projections, and what steps might be taken in order to boost them to the level that the company hopes to achieve. There's also time at the end of each huddle for appreciation, such as praise for an idea that worked out particularly well, or a successful status report. The idea is for people to leave a huddle not only armed with information, but feeling good about the effort they are putting in. They also might depart having agreed that everybody will work toward one intermediate goal and report back the following week.

Open Book Management doesn't mean that every grain of information is shared with every single person in the organization. The idea is to share metrics over which the employees in the room have control, and leave aside issues like the cost of rent or other people's salaries. It's also not a spectator sport. You aren't supposed to go to a huddle and play word games on your phone while other people talk. The aim is for everyone to be financially literate; if there's a term that someone doesn't understand, they're welcome to speak up and ask for an explanation. In the Zingerman's universe, you can't expect people to grasp the numbers if they don't know what the numbers mean. If you think about Zingerman's three goals—great food, great service, and great finances—Open Book is tied into the latter.

Chicago restaurateur Rick Bayless, a devotee of ZingTrain, says he had crafted his own informal version of Open Book Management before he learned the more structured way Zingerman's deployed the concept, but seeing the Zingerman's version helped him hone his approach for his employees, many of whom have little business experience. "It's better if everybody knows what's going on," Bayless says. "The thing we've always done is track our costs. I'm not great at all of that, but I know, having been raised in a family-run restaurant, [that] you have to watch all of that."

SERVANT LEADERSHIP

Servant leadership sounds like an oxymoron. How can you be a servant, if you are also a leader? Isn't the whole idea of leadership to make decisions and have people do what you tell them to do? Yet, if you spend time at Zingerman's, you will quickly see servant leadership in action. It's watching Roadhouse executive chef Bob Bennett help out on the salad line on a busy day, or join the cooks preparing pans of macaroni and cheese. It's seeing chef Kieron Hales, a managing partner at Cornman Farms, one of Zingerman's events spaces, standing at a griddle in the tasting room at the back of Zingerman's Coffee Company, making pancakes on a Saturday morning. (Cornman will be happy to sell you the pancake mix.)

But the person you'll most often see, if you dine at the Roadhouse, is Weinzweig. Weinzweig says his embrace of being visible stems from his personal advancement in the restaurant business at Maude's, from dishwasher to kitchen prep and then to cook. He wound up in a leadership role because he was willing to put in the time and was willing to work harder than anybody else. But like so many people in management, Weinzweig didn't arrive in a position of authority with a great concept of what leadership meant. Remember, his degree is in Russian history, and he didn't have any formal business training. Saginaw, at least, had been a manager, although he chafed at the way other managers treated him. Through trial and error, Weinzweig wanted to come up with an answer to the question "What kind of a leader do I want to be?"

Without that answer, he says, people will never be effective leaders. They'll be wandering around in a haze of frustration—with the world, with staff, with vendors, and eventually with themselves. Barry Sorkin, a co-owner of Smoque BBQ in Chicago, and a big fan of Zingerman's, once told me that a secret he learned running his restaurant was that someone on the staff would always be unhappy, and there would always be a crisis to solve. Managers should never take it personally, but need to make a choice: They can either be consistent leaders, or constantly be trying to put out fires depending on whatever problem came up. Sorkin felt that by being present and approachable, he could keep those issues to a minimum.

Through conversations with his coworkers and partners, Weinzweig settled on the concept of servant leadership. It isn't unique to Zingerman's. The idea comes from the 1977 book *Servant Leadership: A Journey into the Nature of Legitimate Power and Greatness* by Robert K. Greenleaf. According to Greenleaf, servant leadership is "a philosophy and set of practices that enriches the lives of individuals, builds better organizations and ultimately creates a more just and caring world."

The basic belief, according to Weinzweig, is that leaders at Zingerman's are there to serve their organizations, from the managers who run them, to the employees who work in them, to the customers they serve. That might seem obvious, from the term, but it isn't in practice. Usually, service flows from below to above, with leaders benefiting from the efforts of everyone else. Zingerman's begins by treating its staff as "customers" as well as the people who buy its products and services. As a cofounder, Weinzweig's immediate customers are the managing partners, as well as the central administration that reports to him and Saginaw. By turn, the managing partners serve the managers in each of their businesses, and so on.

The idea is that each manager gives great service to the people who report to them, until the energy of this service reaches the frontline staff, like baristas at the coffee company, order takers at the Deli, and the servers at the Roadhouse. This joy then flows out from Zingerman's to its paying customers. "We talk about giving great service to each other, which is how you give great service to others," says Singleton. Anyone at any level of the company at any time can provide service to a paying customer, but the difference is that Zingerman's thinks of its own employees as the equivalent of its guests.

In other words, the better that service flow can be, the better it will be for the entire Zingerman's organization. This is not a concept that everybody in business will be able to embrace, given the hierarchies that exist everywhere from restaurants and retail shops to the floors of car dealerships and beauty salons. Restaurants, in particular, have used a military-style hierarchy for decades, with the executive chef acting as the equivalent of a five-star general. After all, it's hard enough to be a manager. Layer the responsibilities of servant leadership onto that, and you might find it hard for anybody to accept a promotion.

Weinzweig says there might indeed come a time when a manager has to sacrifice something they want for themselves in order to benefit the entire organization. It might be easier to go home early from the Roadhouse than to stay an extra thirty minutes in the kitchen because a family is having a wonderful time and wants to order more food. And, logically, a manager might say, "Wait a minute. I'm paid $75,000 a year to run this restaurant. Why am I giving service to somebody earning tipped wages at $3.67 an hour?," which is the current level in Michigan. But Weinzweig has a good answer for that paradox.

First, he says, servant leadership is simply **the right thing to do.** "Ultimately, it is what we give, not what we get, that defines us as leaders and establishes the legacy that we leave behind in our organizations and our lives," he writes. The proof is in the Zingerman's employees who've risen in the organization to become managers and managing partners at places such as the company's prestigious events venue, Cornman Farms, and Zingerman's Roadhouse (which you'll read about in Chapter 10), or who have used Zingerman's principles to launch their own successful businesses.

One of those food entrepreneurs is Abra Berens, a cookbook writer and chef at Granor Farm in Three Oaks, Michigan, where she creates memorable dinners that feature produce grown only feet from where diners are sitting. She started at the Deli in 2002, and for five years, worked as an order taker and in the kitchen, learning how to handle customers and make matzo ball soup and the vast array of foods in the salad cases. "Zingerman's taught me the how and the why of what I wanted to do," Berens says. "I saw how Zingerman's was committed to playing to people's strengths."

To that end, servant leadership is meant to **help people grow and succeed.** Everybody knows a story of someone who quit because they couldn't stand working for a bad boss. Indeed, 2021 became known as the year of the Great Departure, when millions of employees collectively decided to choose other careers. If people enjoy coming to work because they have a great manager, then it's likely that the organization is going to keep them—or at least, that they'll enjoy the work that they do while they are there.

Weinzweig sees a set of responsibilities for a servant leader. They need to create a vision for the entire staff, like the ones that are described earlier in this chapter. They have to help people understand what the company is going to look like in the short term and the long term. This lets people know what tomorrow is going to look like, and next year, and it eliminates the disorientation a staff member might feel because "I had no idea what to expect from them," he says. In addition, servant leaders have to give great day-to-day service to the staff. They need to manage ethically at all times, treating staff with dignity, showing that they care as individuals, giving up on grudges, and moving forward.

Now, you may nurse grievances from your current job, your past job, even years going back. According to Weinzweig, you've got to let those go. Otherwise, you will be suspended in "an angry, unproductive past." At all times, it's important for a manager to be professional, and responsive— to return phone calls and emails and texts. If a staffer asks for your time, find space on the calendar. Show up on time for meetings or explain why you were late.

Above all, a servant leader expresses thanks. Before the expression "I appreciate you" came into vogue, Weinzweig was saying it to people around him. Years before I started working on this book, I got a text from him one day that said exactly that. Okay, I thought, I don't know what prompted him to write that text. But it made me smile, and now I send my own "I appreciate you" texts and tweets to my friends once in a while, hoping to put a little light into their day.

At Zingerman's, Weinzweig says there are a million ways that managers can thank their employees, like simply saying "thank you" at the end of a shift, paying a compliment, writing a note, and giving gifts of appreciation or recognition. Don't wait for an occasion: Honor them when you see good work, not on an anniversary. Put some joy in their days.

STEPS TO BECOMING A SERVANT LEADER

Here is a system that Weinzweig recommends for practicing servant leadership:

- **Find out what the staff member wants.** Greet them with warmth. Talk to them—more than just a "How's it going?" Keep your ears open. Ask questions, listen well, read their body language and tone of voice.
- **Get it for them.** If there's something a staff member needs, obtain it: (a) accurately (b) politely, and (c) enthusiastically. It's the same thing you'd do with a paying customer.
- **Go the extra mile.** Do something for them they didn't ask for. It could be as simple as buying them coffee, bringing them a cupcake, opening the door for them, just sending a text that says, *It was great to see you do _____ today.*

But every business has problems, and as Sorkin at Smoque BBQ says, there's always going to be somebody who has a complaint. What should a servant leader do when that happens?

- **Acknowledge what they're saying.** Don't start by refuting, or denying, or explaining, or excusing. Just acknowledge that you've heard their concerns. In his case, Weinzweig will say "Oh," or "Wow!" rather than immediately passing judgment.
- **Apologize.** Good managers learn that apologizing can be a useful tool. Some might see it as a diminishing of their power, but it can be just the opposite. A manager who is willing to admit that the employee is entitled to feel upset or bothered could grow in the staff member's eyes. It also can help defuse a tense situation.
- **Make things right.** Maybe checks were late, or the schedule wasn't up. Acknowledge the problem, fix it, and try not to repeat it, just as you'd do with a paying customer.
- **Thank them for complaining.** Again, this is no different than it would be with a paying customer. That is probably going to

catch the employee off guard. But it also tells them that they've been heard, and being heard is a universal comfort. You might think that Zingerman's agonizes when something goes amiss. But you'd be wrong. At Zingerman's, problems are seen to provide "the quickest, clearest path to the future" and a chance to continue to innovate. Says Steve Wallag-Muno, the original Zingerman's graphic artist, "They love problems. They just LOVE problems!"

When you dine at the Roadhouse, you may see Weinzweig moving around the restaurant with a water pitcher. Sometimes, guests just ignore him, and simply go on with their conversations. Other times, people greet him warmly. You might see him reach into his pocket and take out a business card. What does he get out of taking on a job that might normally fall to a busser? In his book *Zingerman's Guide to Good Leading, Part 2,* Weinzweig explained the strategy behind management by pouring water, or MbPW.

First, it is a practical way to approach people's tables, without the drama of "here comes the owner." Wrote Weinzweig, "It was really like a great management gift someone had given me. Pouring water provided an in-the-moment reason to interact with customers." As he found out, no one likes to be left with an empty water glass, so there isn't any pushback when he stops by. Second, he gets to observe buying patterns. Working tables allows him to obtain real-time information about who is ordering what—kids, out-of-towners, regular customers—rather than relying on anecdotes from waitstaff, the kitchen, or checking the nightly order summary.

Third, it's a way to check on process flow. By moving through the dining room, Weinzweig can tell which plates are coming out promptly and which customers are being left waiting. Then he can investigate further to see if it's a server issue or a kitchen one and find a fix. Fourth, he can see whether diners liked the little touches that each dish contained.

Finally, his personal involvement is also crucial in dealing with what Zingerman's calls **moments of truth.** These happen when a customer doesn't complain but makes a mental vow never to come back. Weinzweig, overhearing a server offer a replacement meal, refused to let one grandmother go away unhappy. He suggested a free dessert, and when she resisted, offered her his phone number so they could go out for a walk the next morning. The grandmother and her friends left smiling.

Being on the floor, where staff and customers can see him participate in the night's service, is also an opportunity for Weinzweig to put one of the principles of servant leadership into practice: praise. Complimenting servers, managers, bartenders in front of the customers helps employees feel better and reassures customers that they're in good hands. Weinzweig often introduces new staffers to regulars. That shows the customers they're important and creates a feeling for staff that they work in a place with a solid clientele.

Visioning, Open Book Management, and servant leadership all require thought and effort. But the combination of the three concepts can result in a workplace where managers and staff participate, and customers can see the difference. Weinzweig, however, wanted more guidance to give Zingerman's staff so that they would understand the direction of the business. That fit right in line with Deming's Point No. 14—"Put everyone to work accomplishing the transformation"—and Saginaw says he was happy to have Weinzweig draw up his own set of learning principles.

CHAPTER FIVE

Service on Every Level

Zingerman's is constantly communicating with its customers. There's the Mail Order operation, which ships a thousand packages a day on a slow day and twenty thousand daily during the holidays. If you shop at the Deli or one of its other businesses, you get all sorts of information printed on the paper envelopes that hold croissants and pretzels and the bigger bags used for loaves of bread. Even the shopping bags—pink for small, yellow or transparent in larger sizes—are a source of information. Every purchase from the Deli includes the latest Zingerman's multipage newsletter.

Long before social media put brands in the spotlight, Zingerman's was telling its story verbally, visually, and on paper. "We've always believed we have to give people good reasons to buy from us," Weinzweig says. "If you can't tell them that it's different, why would you buy from us?"

Some of those reasons can be read in the library of books published by Zingerman's Press, which provide explanations of every aspect of its business, from food to philosophy. Some information is specifically about the product in the bag—everything produced at Zingerman's Bakehouse has directions on how best to store it. Then there are the numerous explanatory tags on cheese, meat, olive oil, and other products sold at the Deli, which have been around since the beginning. "You want to be informative. You want to teach people about the product. We're not an educational institution, but we want them to understand why it's meaningful," Weinzweig says.

To be sure, many food companies use packaging to inform their customers about what they sell. On its white shopping bags with distinctive orange-and-brown lettering, Zabar's, the gourmet food store on the Upper West Side of Manhattan, declares that it offers "old time appetizers at Broadway and 80th Street, family run gourmet and epicurean emporium since 1934" followed by a list of dozens of items sold there, from Italian bread sticks and homemade gefilte fish to sesame candy and English Oxford marmalade. A side panel promises, "Great coffee. Guaranteed," while the other panel includes Zabar's website address in bold letters.

However, the most meaningful messages from Zingerman's are delivered by employees themselves, in the service that they give on the phone, in person, and online. Chef Rick Bayless believes that the way Zingerman's interacts with customers is the company's hallmark, more so than the food it serves or the products sold by the Mail Order operation. He likens it to the descriptions that Bayless's servers have always given his customers about the dishes on his menu. "They're telling stories the way we try our best to sell stories," Bayless says. "It's a little harder to tell stories in a restaurant than when you have a captive audience reading your prose." In the Zingerman's approach, "You learn about the products and the dishes and the traditions," he says.

Zingerman's approach to customer service began on the day the Deli opened in 1982, Weinzweig wrote in *Zingerman's Guide to Giving Great Service*. Starting with its quartet of employees, Zingerman's "just did things that seemed incredibly obvious to us: Be really nice to customers and get them what they want—enthusiastically, energetically, and accurately," he said in that book, which was published in 2003.

But as the company grew, he discovered that new employees did not automatically pick up this philosophy from the others they worked with. They also weren't coming up with fresh ideas that could keep Zingerman's unique. It became clear that more formal training was required.

ZINGERMAN'S 12 NATURAL LAWS

If you ever hear him give a presentation, it won't take long for Weinzweig to refer to Zingerman's 12 Natural Laws of Business. They form the canopy under which the company operates, and in a sense, they're the Zingerman's version of Deming's famous points. Weinzweig began compiling them with Saginaw's encouragement, and he has become an evangelist for the ideas. Here's what they include.

1. **A strategically sound vision.** That specifically means the way Zingerman's defines a vision. Says Weinzweig, "To be effective, the vision needs to be so inspiring that everyone involved in achieving it is motivated to contribute their energies. It also needs to be strategically sound. ('As big as we can be as fast as we can get there' is not a vision.')"

2. **Compelling reasons to buy from you.** The way you motivate customers will vary, depending on the type of business, he says. "But if you don't think the reasons your organization is offering sound all that compelling, they probably aren't. So, start working on more."

3. **A great, rewarding place for people to work.** Weinzweig says he's often thought of the people who work at Zingerman's as volunteers—or at least, people who chose to be there over other workplaces. Given that, "How rewarding should the workplace

be? Well, pretty darned rewarding." And by rewarding, he means in every sense of the word—emotionally, intellectually, physically, not just financially. That's the purpose for sharing information like the vision, Open Book Management, and constant training.

4. **Great service to the staff.** That's a basic feature of servant leadership, as you've read earlier. Weinzweig says he can tell "with a high degree of accuracy" how the leaders are treating the staff simply by watching the way much of the staff waits on their customers. "It all starts with us."

5. **Clear expectations and training tools.** The book *First, Break All the Rules*, by Marcus Buckingham and Curt Coffman, featured a Gallup organization survey of one million people, and specifically eighty thousand managers, to determine which factors were most important to keeping the best workers in their jobs for the longest period of time. The single-most-important element in making that happen was clear expectations. The second most critical was tools to do their work, of which effective training (on shift, the job, classroom, online, written, etc.) is a huge piece.

6. **Do things that others don't do.** At the Deli, Weinzweig and Saginaw knew from the start that great bread was a key to the great sandwich that they wanted to serve. They tested loaves from twenty different bakeries and settled on one forty-five minutes away in the Detroit suburbs. But the bakery wouldn't deliver, so someone had to go get the bread and bring it back to Ann Arbor by 7 a.m. Sometimes it was Saginaw, other times it was Ginsberg, who would collect it on the way to making his meat deliveries. "We knew it was worth the effort—and it helped drive our success," Weinzweig says.

7. **Constant improvement.** This is the core of the Toyota production system—the idea of continuous improvement, which, you may recall, is called *kaizen* in Japanese. "The reality of business life is that if we're not learning, growing, and improving, then the marketplace is going to pass us by," Weinzweig says. "The best organizations and individuals have always understood this." Wallag-Muno says he watched that focus up close every day during his thirteen years at the company. "They are constantly trying to make things better," he says.

8. **There will always be problems.** "Would you rather have too few customers and be struggling to pay payroll? Or have sales booming and be struggling to keep up?" Weinzweig asks. Many new businesses aren't experienced enough to maneuver around issues that a veteran company might be able to avoid. But anticipating slipups makes them at least slightly less daunting.

9. **Strength can lead to weakness.** Sometimes, Weinzweig admits, he's tempted "to stick with something longer than I should." The same holds true organizationally. One of Zingerman's strengths is that it has a participative workplace, where ideas are welcomed and thoroughly discussed. However, there are so many chances for people to participate that things take longer than they could have if only one or a few decision makers were involved. But, Weinzweig says, "The beauty of this law is that, if one embraces it rather than fighting it, it actually makes life far less stressful."

10. **Greatness takes time.** Nearly all great organizations and almost all long-term, sustainable successes take a long time to build. Under normal circumstances, Zingerman's requires two years for any meaningful change or new project they undertake to get

to some level of equilibrium. It then takes another year or two to get to be good. And it's only then, Weinzweig says, "that we've got ourselves in position to go after greatness." (This law was especially tested during the pandemic, when Zingerman's didn't have time to waste.)

11. **Profit is good.** Profits alone are not Zingerman's motivator, as I've written previously. But a company *does* have to be profitable to survive, have cash to pay bills, and to cover its taxes and other government obligations. Zingerman's isn't a nonprofit, after all, and it needs to be prosperous in order to share its wealth with employees and the community.

12. **Appreciate your staff, and they'll have more fun.** At Zingerman's, "We've worked hard to create a culture and systems that are positive and appreciative," Weinzweig says. "We're far from perfect and we're certainly not the only ones doing this. But without question, it's contributed enormously to us being the organization that we are." A positive and appreciative workplace setting is much healthier—physically and mentally—for the people who work there.

   This particular law has been borne out by the #MeToo stories that have emerged from the restaurant world over the past few years. The pandemic also highlighted the need for an enjoyable workplace. "Although they'd rather not be struggling, [employees are] glad to at least be struggling with people they really like," Weinzweig says.

While this isn't one of Zingerman's twelve formal points, I'm tempted to add a thirteenth rule, which I would call sharing knowledge. One of the greatest assets that Zingerman's offers is the expertise of its two founders. Saginaw reads books about business concepts the way casual readers consume novels, and he continuously acts as a mentor to countless employees, alumni, and Friends of Zingerman's. Weinzweig has an encyclopedic understanding about the foods that Zingerman's sells and the producers that the company works with. He can expound on subjects like the various cuts of pasta and the sauce that goes best with each of them, the differences between the types of rice produced around the world, every conceivable kind of cheese, and he's right there as a resource for employees.

Far from being an elusive founder, Weinzweig is often among the first people employees get to meet at the first training class they take, and this instruction is another asset that sets Zingerman's apart from ordinary small companies.

BOTTOM LINE TRAINING

At the start of their employment, Zingerman's staff members are taught two concepts: Bottom Line Training and Bottom Line Change. They were created to convince employees that they played a vital role in the company and help them see the results of their participation. These concepts are in addition to the three bottom lines—good food, good service, and good finances—that compose a basic Zingerman's belief. Yes, it's a lot of bottom lines, but the concepts intersect.

As Zingerman's embraced employee training, it wasn't out to give employees skills just so they'd learn something; Zingerman's also wanted to know that the training was effective. In Bottom Line Training, it came up with five priorities for the benefits it was trying to reap.

First, it wanted training that was simple and quick to implement. Second, it focused on the problem areas as they came up. Third, it provided information that staff needed to know in order to successfully do their jobs. Fourth, it created tools that would reduce—not increase—the burden on leadership. And finally, the training staff members received had to have a positive impact on one of Zingerman's three bottom lines that I talked about earlier in the book, meaning food, service, or finances.

The five training priorities fit nicely with Zingerman's Visioning concept. Visioning teaches the destination, while Bottom Line Training begins to fill in the blanks. There are two main components. The first is the **training compact.** This lays out roles for teachers and students, or in staff terms, managers (called trainers at ZingTrain), and employees. In it, the supervisors agree to document clear expectations, provide resources needed for training, recognize performance, and reward it.

It isn't simply managers or trainers lecturing and employees listening silently. They're expected to ask lots of questions and give feedback on whether they have what they need to improve. Zingerman's managers and trainers bear 100 percent of the responsibility for making sure that the instruction is effective. In turn, the trainee is 100 percent responsible for telling them whether it has been. Nobody walks away mystified.

The second piece of the system is Zingerman's **Four Training Plan Questions,** which identify the information that the organization needs to provide to employees to ensure that they can be successful.

The questions are:

1. What is expected of the trainee—and by when?
2. How will that information be made available, and what kind of resources are available?
3. How will people know that expectations are being met—or are not being met?
4. What are the rewards for meeting expectations, and the consequences if they are not met?

Each newly hired employee receives a "training passport," created by ZingTrain's original managing partner, Maggie Bayless, which specifically spells out their job requirements and the knowledge they are expected to acquire. Here's how the introduction to each one reads:

WELCOME TO YOUR TRAINING PASSPORT!

Why We Use Training Passports

✤ They clarify what your manager expects you to know and by when—no one expects you to know everything in your 1st week!

✤ They give you the resources to complete orientation at your own pace—we expect [completion] within **90 days from your hire date**

✤ They empower you to take responsibility for your training—take the lead and ask your trainers to cover what's in your passport

Tips for Completing YOUR Training Passport

✤ **Review** each line on your passport and ask your manager if you have questions of clarification

✤ **Ask** your trainers to sign off on each line as you complete the on-shift training

✤ **Review** the ZCoB Class Calendar; ask your manager how to request time to attend the classes you need

✤ **Sign up** for classes that fit in your schedule; RSVP to the instructor

✤ **ASK FOR HELP** if you can't fit a class you need into your schedule

✦ **Know** the location of each class; ask for help if you are confused

✦ **Take** Food Safety within 60 days or you'll be taken off the schedule until you do

✦ **Keep** your passport intact—if you lose it, get a replacement from your manager

✦ **Turn it in** to your manager once you've completed all the tasks & have gotten them signed off

Why Completing Orientation Is Good For YOU! *(The following benefits aren't available for Temporary or Occasional staff)*:

✦ *PTO* (Paid Time Off); the sooner you complete orientation, the more PTO you'll have available to you when you complete eligibility requirements

✦ If you're **FULL-TIME**, you'll *receive an additional PTO day* if you complete orientation within **90 days from your hire date**

✦ Get *a discount card* and receive discounts all around the ZCoB

✦ Sign up for *UofZ programs* that offer monetary awards after completion

✦ Receive $30 towards the cost of *Slip Grips* (slip-resistant shoes)

✦ Get reimbursed for 25% of the cost of a *massage* from a certified therapist

✦ Receive a *Free BAKE! Class* coupon

The actual training passports differ according to each part of the company, but you can see a complete one for Zingerman's Bakehouse in Chapter 10.

BOTTOM LINE CHANGE

Bottom Line Change is the process that Zingerman's came up with to ensure that it implemented long-lasting and effective change, explains Katie Frank, managing partner for ZingTrain. The impact is designed to be meaningful on its three bottom lines: great food, great service, and great finances. "If the change doesn't directly impact one of those three, we don't do it," Frank says.

Bottom Line Change is more than a suggestion box, for one key reason. Although anybody at Zingerman's is empowered to bring up an idea, once they do so, they are tasked with taking ownership of it and figuring out whether it can be implemented. "It doesn't mean that every change proposed goes through, and that's okay," Frank says. "We want staff thinking like leaders." If the idea doesn't happen, Zingerman's managers will work with staff to see how the idea could be strengthened and implemented in the future.

As with other organizational change processes, Zingerman's problem-solving concept breaks the process of creating a new practice into an eight-step "recipe," which is accompanied by three follow-up steps. First, there needs to be a **clear and compelling purpose** for the change. This involves collecting data and getting agreement that things need to be done differently. Second, the change seeker creates a vision of **what things would look like** when a change takes place, and gets leaders to buy in. Third, those involved figure out **who needs to know**, and be involved in the change. Fourth, the **vision is presented**, and those involved provide feedback and suggestions. Fifth, **it is implemented**. Once those five steps from conception to implementation are achieved, Bottom Line Change includes three follow-up steps to gauge success, in which employees "adjust, celebrate, and document" the change.

Here's an example of how Zingerman's puts Bottom Line Change to work. During the week, the menu at Zingerman's Roadhouse includes blue plate specials, which vary based on the time of day. They're advertised on big round placards that hang above the Roadhouse's open kitchen, with morning dishes on one side, afternoon dishes on the other. The breakfast versions came about from a suggestion by Laura Fulton, a veteran server who worked the early shift, which typically drew fewer customers than lunch or dinner. She had an idea to generate more breakfast business for the Roadhouse, which would lead to more revenue—and more tips. This constituted a "clear and compelling reason" for the change. So she met with Tabitha Mason, then a manager at the Roadhouse, and suggested a daily deal.

As they figured out possible menu items, Mason asked Fulton to calculate how many she thought they could sell, what the cost of raw ingredients would be, how to price the specials, and how they should be marketed—the data collection portion of the process. Then the kitchen staff, which naturally needed to provide input on how Fulton's idea would be implemented, joined the conversation. Roadhouse cooks came up with the simplest methods to produce the specials so they did not hinder the flow of the breakfast line.

The specials, such as a smothered breakfast burrito, breakfast tacos, and biscuits and gravy—were added first to the breakfast menu and tested to see which resonated with customers. Once it was clear the specials were hits, lunch items were created. The daily specials affected Zingerman's food, by offering new menu options; they affected its service, by giving staff an opportunity to earn more at what had been a slower time; and they helped its finances, by expanding the menu. The Roadhouse keeps track of how many are ordered, and people on the staff know that they were Fulton's idea, which serves as an inspiration to come up with more types of Bottom Line Change.

Here's an example of how a Bottom Line Change suggestion looks in the actual Zingerman's format (condensed and clarified):

ZINGERMAN'S ROADHOUSE NEW JUICER BLC, AKA "BIG DUDE"

COMPELLING REASONS:

1. The juicer we have now is broken.

2. Each bar employee spends one to three hours nightly slicing and juicing fruit. A new juicer can produce 100 quarts of juice in 90 minutes.

3. Our juicing (production) is currently 40 quarts. With a new juicer, we can produce 40 quarts in 35 minutes.

4. Three hours a night manually producing juice costs $6,550 a year on labor costs. Producing juice with the new juicer will cut labor costs in half and save $3,200 a year!

5. Yield of juice per orange should increase, too!

VISION:

It's the end of summertime, and fresh squeezed juices and mimosas are selling like crazy. We feature them more and more on menus, drink specials, etc. In fact, we now have a couple of Roadhouse drink specials that are based on fresh juice. Servers now push fresh juice at lunch and dinner, too, and many of our non-alcohol-consuming guests love it. We've also started to do limeade, since we can handle fresh limes in the machine.

MICROCOSM:
WHO NEEDS TO KNOW?

1. All bar staff, management, Roadshow and back of the house.

2. Bar customers: we should tell them before it comes, and regularly give them fresh tastes of juice to get them to like it.

HOW DO WE LET THEM KNOW?

1. Have a bar meeting, discuss the new machine, and how the work will change.
2. A draft version of the B.L.C. is emailed (to staff), talked about in pre-shift meetings, discussed at all chef and management meetings, and talk to each bar staff individually.

Action steps:

Order the juicer

Install the juicer

Check juice costs to make sure prices are high enough

File the product manuals where they can be easily found

Make sure it's clear where to go for maintenance needs

Meet 30 days after we get it to review how it's going

(Postscript from me: the limeade is delicious)

Zingerman's overarching philosophy, and the way that it trains and encourages its employees, all have been key elements in building the enterprise. But long before Zingerman's got as big as it is now, Saginaw and Weinzweig had to make some crucial, and ultimately unusual, decisions about the organizational structure they wanted.

PART THREE

Inside Zingerman's

Until the pandemic, Zingerman's customers lined up to order sandwiches with quirky names like "Who's Greenberg, Anyway?" (a nod to what they wanted to call the Deli). (Courtesy of Zingerman's)

CHAPTER SIX

A Community of Businesses

Visiting Ann Arbor, out-of-towners quickly realize that the University of Michigan is everywhere. There's the main campus, with its stately classical buildings, and fancier new ones, named for billionaire benefactors like Charlie Munger, Warren Buffett's right-hand man, and the late real estate developer A. Alfred Taubman. A few miles away sits North Campus, built in the last half of the twentieth century, home to the schools of architecture, engineering, music, and much of the university's research. Then, scattered across town, are individual buildings and administrative offices, some of which pop up unexpectedly in Ann Arbor's leafy neighborhoods.

Zingerman's is now something like that. Many people think only of the original Deli in Kerrytown. But that site alone now encompasses four buildings, while Zingerman's operations elsewhere within the city limits include the Roadhouse, as well as Greyline, an event space in part of a reclaimed bus depot. Zingerman's Mail Order takes up two long buildings in an office park on the south side of Ann Arbor, while the collection of businesses called Zingerman's South encompasses another set of industrial park buildings about a mile away. Beyond Ann Arbor, Zingerman's operates Cornman Farms in rural Dexter, Michigan, about a twenty-minute drive from the Deli. Zingerman's bread is available at a variety of locations, and Zingerman's products abound at Plum Market grocery stores, including an outpost at Detroit Metropolitan Airport. The assortment of locations is a bit of a patchwork, and any other company might have looked to consolidate most of the businesses in one spot. Certainly, given the farmland and other available property that surrounds Ann Arbor, a commercial developer would have happily built a single complex that could fit all of Zingerman's manufacturing and back-office needs. But the scattered operations reflect the unusual approach that Zingerman's took to growth, as well as its idea of governance, when deciding to add new ventures to its portfolio and embracing the idea of a community of businesses. Asked about the way things turned out, Saginaw says, "We never knew it would get this big."

CREATING ZCOB

In 1994, Saginaw and Weinzweig decided that instead of franchising Zingerman's or replicating the Deli themselves, Zingerman's could become a bigger enterprise unto itself. They crafted the idea of a community of businesses, or ZCoB for short. In the vision document they published that year, called Zingerman's 2009, they hoped they could create as many as fifteen businesses, with revenue quadrupling from $5 million in 1994 to about $20 million annually fifteen years later. (Needless to say, they were far too conservative on where Zingerman's revenue eventually wound up.)

The cofounders were not looking to invent an entirely new corporate structure, nor did they want an old-style, top-down organizational chart with a hierarchy that controlled everything. They described the ZCoB model as planets orbiting around a sun, but it actually is similar to the Japanese system called *keiretsu*. In it, a parent company, like Toyota, oversees a variety of related businesses, like steel, glassmaking, and plastic molding. These individual firms report profits and losses, and supply their parent as well as external customers, just as many of the Zingerman's businesses have done. You can see this in the way the Bakehouse supplies the Deli, Mail Order, and the Roadhouse, or the way Mail Order scoops up products from across ZCoB, marketing them alongside other goods.

ZCoB also found inspiration from a company closer to home: Ford. In the 1920s and 1930s, Henry Ford set up the "village industries" across southeast Michigan. His idea was to place Ford operations in small towns, like Northville, Saline, Dundee, and Brooklyn. In the beginning, these power plants and little factories provided manufacturing jobs to farmers once the harvest was over and before spring planting began. ZCoB didn't have that kind of seasonal aspect, but under the community of business umbrella, the Zingerman's collective established individual leaders, called managing partners, in charge of each business. Each company is responsible for its own financial performance. Then the results are calculated across ZCoB to reflect how the whole company is doing. Open Book Management allows everyone across Zingerman's to get a picture of how each business unit is performing. The businesses are designed to share and learn best practices among each other, so that the Zingerman's philosophy resounds throughout the organization.

Originally, Saginaw and Weinzweig ranked at the top as cofounders, and owned pieces of every enterprise through a holding company set up when the Deli began. But they felt the managing partner concept was crucial. For one thing, they didn't want to stretch themselves too thin or constantly deal with problems that on-site managers could better address. They also wanted others to participate because they knew it would make a difference to customers. "When the owner is on-site, there's a different energy and a different feel," Weinzweig says. "If I help you, I'm helping myself, and if I help myself, I'm helping you."

Other cofounders might prefer to keep a tighter grip, but Saginaw says he and Weinzweig shared an abundance mentality. "Once you're in a position where you're not worried about keeping the roof over your head, I don't think an enormous amount of money brings you any more joy," he says. "If you let go of that, it's liberating. It gives you a sense of freedom to be generous, to innovate, to share. That's the fun of having a big giant resource that a business can be and how much good do you do with it."

THE PATH TO PARTNERSHIP

There has been no "one size fits all" approach to selecting the managing partners. Saginaw and Weinzweig were and remain open-minded on the type of résumé that a partner should have. While some managing partners have MBAs and years of experience in corporate and other restaurant company jobs, a business credential is not required—no surprise given that neither of the founders has formal financial training. Quips Weinzweig: "Sometimes I don't understand what the accountants are saying." Initially, they thought each business would have one managing partner, but as Zingerman's expanded over the past thirty years, some businesses had two or three managing partners, to share the investment risk as well as the workload.

By 2021, the company had twenty-three managing partners, and with some of Zingerman's longest-serving partners retiring, it was likely that more new faces would imminently be added to the group. Early on, Saginaw says the idea was to give opportunities solely to existing Zingerman's managers. "We wanted to be places where people would find their passion," he says. But as sales grew and the workloads became heavier, managers were hired from other restaurant companies, as well as completely different types of businesses. Some leaders took on multiple duties. In addition to serving as a cofounder, Weinzweig is the managing partner for the Roadhouse, while Steve Mangigian has responsibility for two companies, Coffee and Candy. But, Cornman Farms, the events space, has two managing partners of its own, while the Deli and Mail Order have three.

Anyone within the organization can voice their interest in eventually becoming a partner. They must write a vision for what they think a new business can be, or what an existing business can evolve into. The initial outline is only a start; it can take years to hone a vision for a new venture, with feedback from Weinzweig and Saginaw, as well as other partners. And, even if the type of business they are proposing is among those mentioned in the overall company vision, that doesn't mean it will come to pass. For instance, Zingerman's has been mulling a brewery for years. But a Zingerman's craft beer company would face competitive hurdles. Ann Arbor has a number of independent breweries, and other cities across Michigan have hundreds of breweries and brew pubs. As with the Deli's sandwiches, a Zing Brewery would have to be great, and thus far, that hasn't happened.

Once a prospective partner's candidacy is accepted, they go through an eighteen-month course called path to partnership, which educates them about Zingerman's management philosophy and teaches them about each of the business units. Each is assigned a "sherpa," the company's term for another managing partner of whom they can ask questions and get advice. Zingerman's puts up some of the investment, while each managing partner is ideally supposed to contribute, but the percentage of their investment varies, depending on the type of business and the revenues that it produces. Some, like Allen Leibowitz, the original partner at Zingerman's Coffee, wanted to own their company outright. "I came in completely capitalized," he says. But he says he was told, "We don't do that." So, he took a 50 percent share, and Weinzweig and Saginaw owned the other half through the entity they set up for their Zingerman's holdings.

By contrast, Tabitha Mason, a managing partner at Cornman Farms, had no money to put up in order to become one of Cornman's two partners, but that was not an obstacle to her candidacy. Mason's journey to partnership began in 2011, when she joined Zingerman's Roadhouse as general manager. She spent sixteen years at the Bavarian Inn, one of Michigan's most famous restaurants, in Frankenmuth, about a hundred miles north of Detroit. Owned by the Zehnder family, which also operates a restaurant under its own name, the Bavarian Inn specializes in serving vast platters of fried chicken and German specialties. At peak pre-pandemic tourist times, five thousand guests could come through the door on any one day.

Mason loved working there, but she also enjoyed her family trips to Ann Arbor, where a visit to the Deli was always on the itinerary. Even if the family didn't eat on-site, they'd pick up food to go. Mason's decision to join Zingerman's resulted from a passing remark by her daughter. As the young woman's high school graduation approached, Mason told her daughter that she had been voted "most daring" by her classmates. Her daughter replied, "What have you ever done that was daring?" That made Mason think, "What am I doing here? And so, I simply applied [at the Roadhouse] on a whim."

For anyone else, the prospect of walking into the Roadhouse as a general manager might be daunting. But because of her high-volume Frankenmuth experience, Mason thought she was prepared for the crowds that the Roadhouse regularly welcomed. "Being able to stand and look into every room, I was like, 'This is so easy, and I won't get it wrong,'" Mason recalls. She quickly learned that Roadhouse customers arrived expecting something special, beyond the abundant platters of food that the Bavarian Inn placed on its guests' tables.

As she delved deeper into her job, Mason became fascinated by the idea of Open Book Management, having experienced the opposite years before. When she was pregnant with her first child, her husband arrived at the restaurant where he worked to find the doors bolted shut. Eventually, the building reverted to the bank to pay off the owner's debt. Although he ranked second in the hierarchy behind the owner, he had no idea that the restaurant was in such dire financial straits.

"It was devastating for our family," Mason says. "I didn't know what Open Book was, but I knew that I never wanted to be in that position again. As a leader, I would do everything in my power to make sure I wasn't going to be someone who would do that to another person."

When she began working at the Roadhouse, Mason attended her first huddle, a key part of the way each ZCoB business operates. Based on her Bavarian Inn experience, she envisioned a routine review of how the restaurant was faring, and perhaps some discussion of new dishes that might join the menu. But at Zingerman's, a huddle is a far more comprehensive event. She heard staff members talking about labor costs, revenue, where money should be spent, and where it could be saved. She also saw how staffers were encouraged, through Bottom Line Change, to come up with ideas that would benefit the organization.

"I was like, 'Yeah, this is what I've been missing,'" Mason says of the brainstorming process.

After several years at the Roadhouse, Mason briefly worked at the company's shared services operation, formally called Zingerman's Service Network, or ZingNet for short. (The name was changed in 2021 to Zing IP, LLC.) It oversees information technology, financial operations, marketing and human resources functions, and hosts three company committees that oversee training, safety, and benefits. Mason's position there was called service steward, and her duties included teaching classes on service, working with individual parts of the company on service topics, and chairing Zingerman's Great Service committee. She began to think about advancement.

"What brought me here was the idea of giving great service to the staff. And I loved hearing about servant leadership," she says. "But I realized that my impact on employees and the community around me would be greater if I were an owner instead of an employee." Her realization coincided with a similar one experienced by a Roadhouse coworker. Kieron Hales's restaurant career began in England, when he was accepted at the Royal Academy of Culinary Arts at age thirteen. His travels took him to twenty-seven different countries, including stints at Paul Bocuse's

Michelin three-star restaurant in France; Dal Pescatore Santini, outside Mantua, Italy; and the opportunity to cook for members of the British Royal Family as well as three U.S. presidents. He emigrated to the United States in 2008, where he joined Zingerman's, becoming the executive chef at the Roadhouse, and a jovial presence.

In 2013, Zingerman's, with backing from a group of investors, purchased a forty-two-acre working farm in Dexter, Michigan, about fifteen miles from Ann Arbor. Set amid rolling fields outside the quaint small town, the property had barns and an elegant white farmhouse built in 1934, but it needed a thorough renovation to compete with other upscale events venues. For the previous three years, Hales had been crafting a vision that called for transforming Cornman into a place to hold weddings and corporate events like the ride-and-drive programs that car companies host to show off new vehicles, as well as a location to grow food.

Hales had proposed becoming sole managing partner, overseeing all the cuisine and activities. "One hundred percent, the reason he came to America was because he wanted to own a business," Mason says. But as the project was taking shape, it was clear that Cornman was going to need more than one person running it, so Hales suggested Mason might consider taking part. Mason went to see Saginaw to discuss the idea. She felt that her strengths and Hales's could mesh. The workload divided naturally between Mason's management skills and Hales's culinary expertise, with Mason taking charge of events and Hales crafting and cooking the menus. Saginaw encouraged her to move forward.

It cost Zingerman's about $800,000 to acquire the property, she says, and another $4.2 million was needed for its development, including a complete renovation of the farmhouse to house a commercial kitchen, restoration of the barns, and landscaping, among other steps. While Mason did not have capital available, Hales invested an inheritance from his parents, and the venture raised $3.8 million from outside funders, many of them local residents who were longtime Zingerman's admirers.

GETTING ADVICE

For her first year, Mason's sherpa was Toni Morell, one of three managing partners at Mail Order. Steve Mangigian says selecting a new partner's sherpa receives serious consideration by the other partners, since that person will be responsible for the newcomer's assimilation and growth. "It's not for grandstanding. It's for bringing someone along," Mangigian says. In her case, says Mason, "It was really good to have someone I could call and just say, 'Do I talk too much? Do I not talk enough? If I have an opinion, how do I share it?' You sort of learn to navigate the relationship securely enough."

A number of the twenty-three managing partners have been with Zingerman's for twenty years or more. Thus, sherpas are a bridge when younger partners are feeling their way into the structure. "There's a lot of time as a new partner when you're in the room, and you're like, 'I feel there's something going on that I don't understand,'" Mason says. "Someone is telling a story about something that happened twenty years ago, and I can't ask right now, but I want to make sure I figure out what's going on with that story."

Even if the more recent participants sometimes can get lost figuring out Zingerman's practices, Mangigian says the newest partners energize the veterans. "Everyone is on fire to contribute, add value, add ideas." He welcomes having fresh eyes review the company's financial results, which are distributed to staff on a monthly basis. "I don't think I'd even know how to run a company without Open Book Management anymore," Mangigian says.

Weinzweig says that becoming the managing partner of the Roadhouse has given him a new view of the company he helped start in 1982. "It's been helpful for me to reground in the day-to-day work of the managing partner," he says. "I don't think I was unempathetic, but it's more a reminder of how hard it is to get anything done. When the cooler's breaking, and six people call in sick and two people quit, it's hard to get time to talk to people."

A COMPLEX OWNERSHIP STRUCTURE

Although it may seem that Zingerman's can sometimes be slow to move on important steps, adopting new concepts is the norm inside the organization during its forty-year life-span. ZCoB itself has been through a series of modifications since the idea was originally implemented in 1994, reflecting Zingerman's unusual financial structure. Even though ZCoB seems like the ownership umbrella for the organization, it does not function that way. Zingerman's actual structure is complicated. The majority of ownership still rests with Weinzweig and Saginaw. They primarily hold their shares of Zingerman's Deli and in each business through Dancing Sandwich Enterprises, classified as a C corporation. Their holdings might range from 20 percent to 80 percent of each business, depending on the shares they took.

Originally, each business paid a licensing fee to Dancing Sandwich for its use of the Zingerman's brand, which was how Weinzweig and Saginaw were paid (neither took a salary from any of the subsidiary companies). Dancing Sandwich owns the trademarks on more than thirty different Zingerman's practices and business units, including the Deli, Zingermans.com, Bottom Line Training, Bake!, Greyline, and Camp Bacon. Meanwhile, the Deli and its surrounding buildings are the property of another LLC, while other real estate such as Mail Order is owned by a different subsidiary.

But things began to change in 2007. That year, in a vision written for 2020, Zingerman's vowed that it would find a way to share the growth and financial opportunity of ZCoB among staff. That wasn't possible through Dancing Sandwich, and since each of the individual businesses was created as LLCs, they could not become employee owed, either. It took six years of deliberation by its governance committee until Zingerman's created an additional channel called Zingerman's Experience, LLC. It was launched in 2015, for the express purpose of sharing ownership and wealth across ZCoB.

Each person who had been at Zingerman's for a year could purchase one share for $1,000. If they did not have the money up front, Zingerman's lent it to them, with the debt paid off via payroll deduction. Ownership made them eligible to take part in a special company-wide profit-sharing program, in addition to any profit sharing that their own company offered. The payout kicked in when ZCoB achieved a 2 percent net profit across its businesses. The expectation was that within several years, employees would be reimbursed the cost of their shares via the distributions. "We wanted them to be looking less at their own business, and looking more at the Community of Businesses," Saginaw says. "I think there's a psychological difference."

About four hundred employees decided to take part in the inaugural year, including Saginaw and Weinzweig, who each bought a share. In 2016, the first year a payout was offered, each shareholder received a dividend of $309. Subsequent annual payouts ranged from nothing, when the ZCoB-wide profit target was not achieved, to about $200 a year. By 2021, the number of shareholders had fallen below two hundred, due to pandemic-related departures, as well as typical turnover, says Ron Maurer, Zingerman's chief administrative officer. Despite the pandemic, however, shareholders got some compensation for 2020. Mail Order was so successful due to a flood of business that a share of its profits was used to make that year's $175 payout. By then, a shareholder who stuck with the program throughout its lifetime had earned dividends of $867, Maurer says. Meanwhile, a $500 payout, the highest that can be distributed, was slated for the 2021 fiscal year. That meant that anyone from the original group who still held their $1,000 share now had recouped their investment, plus a profit. These shares cannot be sold to anyone outside Zingerman's and are bought back by the LLC at the $1,000 face value when the employee leaves.

Zingerman's also created a new level of nonownership partnerships called staff (or resident) partners, who are elected by the Zingerman's Experience shareholders. These three employees join the management partners for two years. They must write a vision for a project they would like to explore. At the end of their tenure, they present their findings to a management huddle, and the information is distributed to the shareholders.

"What we've learned over the past couple of years is that there are people who want to invest, but don't necessarily want to become managing partners," Mason says. "And our current structure doesn't allow them to grow. In general, you [become a managing partner] because you think, 'This is my business. It's going to be here for decades.' And that isn't for everyone. Someone might be here a short time, and they might want to have a business."

THE ADVANTAGES OF OPEN GOVERNANCE

While Zingerman's organizational structure allows for advancement and participation, it also can seem a little convoluted, especially if you compare it with public or private companies of similar size. A $65 million public company might have a board, management, and shareholders; a privately held company, such as a family business, would be in the hands of a few people, with everyone else simply on staff.

Mangigian, who worked for a family-owned company before joining Zingerman's, prefers the transparency here. At his old firm, "we operated in absolute secrecy. We never told staff anything about our numbers. The only way staff knew they were doing well was if they got a bonus at the end of the year." He says the partnership structure creates "a fundamental difference" between Zingerman's and other companies its size. "We don't go after businesses. We go after people," Mangigian says. "There is something here for everyone. We require people to drive their own growth and future. That's what I really like."

Says Weinzweig, "We have a lot of governance, and that's a rare thing, especially at this scale." He realizes Zingerman's model is unique and might not be applicable everywhere. Once in a while, he jokes, he wonders what would happen among the managing partners if Martians swooped down from the sky and captured Zingerman's. "They'd meet at the partners group, somebody would write a vision for how it was going to go, and they'd have the values, so they'd need to know what to do."

CHAPTER SEVEN

Mail Order

The Zingerman's Mail Order catalog is not just for people interested in shopping for food, but for those who enjoy reading about it, too. That's a lot of people. The catalog has two million addresses on its mailing list, while about a hundred thousand people order something from Zingerman's in a typical year. Mail Order is by far the biggest of Zingerman's businesses, about five times larger than the Deli in terms of revenue. It did about $27 million in sales in fiscal 2021, roughly 41 percent of ZCoB's overall revenue. In total, Zingerman's four biggest businesses—Mail Order, the Bakehouse, the Deli, and the Roadhouse—comprised about 85 percent of the company's revenue. "It's a whole different ball of wax. It's such a Zingerman's machine," says Wallag-Muno, who drew the first mailing flyer.

Mail Order is the primary way that people outside Ann Arbor become part of the Zingerman's food community. "Before I ever visited Ann Arbor and knew Ari, I got the Zingerman's catalog," says John T. Edge at Southern Foodways. "It was like Ari and a band of sherpas went off into the world and brought it back to you." Says the Deli's Rick Strutz: "Mail Order is what takes us and gets us out of the community. It allows us to do business in lots and lots of other places." During the pandemic, cookbook author Molly Stevens says Mail Order allowed her to stay connected to the retail world. "I order a sweater, and I have no place to wear it. So, I'm treating myself to a little extra nut oil."

Zingerman's Mail Order wasn't officially one of the first ZCoB businesses, but it was one of the earliest things that Zingerman's did beyond the walls of the Deli. As far back as the 1980s, customers would call the Deli and place orders to be shipped, says Mo Frechette, one of Mail Order's three managing partners. In the late 1980s, Zingerman's began mailing out flyers drawn by Wallag-Muno that featured some of the items that could be delivered. In 1993, it sent out its first Mail Order catalog. Saginaw says Weinzweig wasn't sold on the idea: "That was something that other people did," Saginaw says. But Frechette and another Zingerman's employee, Jude Walton, were enthusiastic, and eventually became Mail Order's first managing partners.

When the original catalog was published, Zingerman's did not anticipate becoming a mass marketer of its own goods; it saw the catalog primarily as a way to sell the gourmet items that it obtained from other places. "The only manufacturing business was the bakery, and there was not a single thought in my head that we would be a [baked-goods] baking shipping company," Frechette says. At that time, Mail Order was so small that a mention of one of its items in a national magazine or newspaper would result in a bump of telephone calls. Frechette says he could tell when Zingerman's had gotten some publicity, like a mention in the *New York Times'* weekly Dining section or an item featured in *Gourmet* magazine. "People would call up and ask to be put on our mailing list. Somebody would write their name down," he says. "We had a tiny, tiny phone bank" with about eight lines open. Eventually, Zingerman's gained the capacity to take a hundred calls at a time. And then the internet came along.

Zingermans.com was launched in 1999 by Tom Root and Toni Morell, now managing partners with Frechette at Mail Order. "At some point, we stopped being a business that relied on luck to get a new customer, and learned the nuts and bolts of direct marketing," Frechette says.

As it did so, a pattern emerged at Mail Order. The catalog was divided equally between products Zingerman's made itself and those that it curated from other food producers. Mail Order had two basic seasons: the thirty days before Christmas and the rest of the year, and the contrast was vivid. Half its annual business occurred during the period from Thanksgiving to Christmas, and the other half was distributed over the remaining eleven months. Pre-pandemic, Zingerman's took about a thousand mail orders per day, perhaps less during the summer. That swelled to as many as twenty thousand orders per day during the holidays, and there was rarely a day between Thanksgiving and Christmas with fewer than four thousand orders, Frechette says. In the first six months of the pandemic, business surged to "levels we'd never seen in the off-season," with orders up 100 to 200 percent year over year, and demand continued to be strong in the months that followed.

Much like the Deli itself, Zingerman's catalog abounds with multi-colored cartoons, drawings of products, and enticing copy for every one of the products inside. Frechette says about half its sales are of Zingerman's own goods, and about half from other vendors. The holiday catalog ran fifty-six pages for the 2020 Christmas season, each page abounding with information. Yet the approach is down-to-earth. The catalog is printed on a matte newsprint-like stock called Roland Opaque Smooth, with 30 percent recycled material, not the glossy sheets that other catalogs use, and the descriptions, written by Frechette and other catalog staff, are upbeat. Despite its sophisticated audience, Frechette says Zingerman's doesn't assume the reader already is familiar with a product. Instead, they describe it in mouth-watering fashion. "We start from zero," he says. "We tell people, 'You might like to try this.'" But he adds, "We never write stuff that's not true."

Take babka, which came in two varieties in 2020: chocolate raisin and date fig pomegranate. "Babka is a sweet loaf, both fluffy and rich, kind of like a light-textured coffee cake with a dense filling swirled throughout," the catalog copy read. "The master bakers at Zingerman's

Bakehouse make two flavors of babka. The first is swirling with chocolate and cinnamon and studded with juicy golden sultana raisins. The second is balanced between sweet and tart, loaded with earthy dates, luscious figs and bright pomegranate molasses swirled throughout, and topped with slivered almonds. Wrapped in tissue and gift boxed, each serves 6–8." The babkas, a popular gift item, were priced at forty-five dollars, with free shipping. On other pages, you'll find headlines declaring "Rare Sweet Treats" and "Classic Never-Fail Gifts."

Catalog copy like that takes plenty of time and imagination to create. "They're very serious about it," says Saginaw. Frechette says the copywriters are working on every page right until the catalog is printed and mailed out. "I find that is the hallmark of a lot of good books and magazines," he says. "The *Simpsons* writers write those shows until the last possible second. That kind of constant attention to detail shows up. We sweat the details over and over. It's what a business has to do." Even when a food producer has been repeatedly included in the catalog, the descriptions of its wares still vary, depending on the time of year and the length of the catalog blurb. For Nueske's bacon, one of the first items that Zingerman's sold, there are long and short write-ups, a Father's Day version, and ones that reintroduce popular products like Applewood smoked bacon.

Even though Nueske's can be found at the Deli, in supermarkets, and in specialty stores in many parts of the United States, Mail Order still sells a lot of it. The catalog's most popular sellers are items from the Bakehouse—the ones Frechette never dreamed Mail Order would sell because they're perishable—such as coffee cakes, which are the single-biggest revenue generator. Koeze's Cream-Nut peanut butter, made in Grand Rapids, Michigan, also sells well. So do sandwich kits, like one for the Reuben that President Obama ordered. Its box includes bread, meat, cheese, Russian dressing, sauerkraut, potato chips, brownies, and instructions on how to craft a sandwich.

But less expensive items do well, too. Each year, Mail Order sells about 80,000 to 100,000 tins of Ortiz tuna from Spain. It starts at nine dollars a tin (seven dollars if you buy four or more; a case of thirty costs $200). Why is it so popular? For one thing, the drawings are fun, and the price is reasonable. For another, "it is exceptional fish," Frechette says. "I've tasted hundreds of tinned fish. There are some that are better, but the ones that are better cost triple." Here's how the tuna is described in the catalog, as told by Mail Order manager Brad Hedeman:

Here in the U.S., tinned tuna is a low-end commodity usually sold in supermarkets. In Spain it's at the complete opposite of the culinary spectrum. Writing in the *New Yorker,* Lauren Collins said Spain is "perhaps the only country in the world where it is desirable to serve food that comes in a can."

Tuna in tins, especially these from the fourth-generation family firm Ortiz, is one of the jewels in Spain's culinary crown. Ortiz's fish are all line caught—not netted—hand cleaned and tinned in good olive oil. The olive oil is key. It adds flavor and makes the texture silky over time.

Bonito—or albacore, as it's commonly known in America— is the most mellow and highly prized species. It gets my vote for top everyday eating tuna. It's nearly the ultimate in convenience food. A quick turn of the lid, and you can serve it with salads, beans, appetizer platters or on its own, dressed with some top-notch olive oil, a squeeze of lemon and a sprinkling of sea salt.

Decades ago, chefs used to select their preferred tuna batches at Ortiz. But it fell out of favor, and no one has done it for years— until we did. Recently Mo and Brad went to Getaria, a fishing village in northern Spain off the Bay of Biscay, to taste all the batches of tuna that Ortiz had tinned for America. We nabbed the most flavorful, a single shoal that resulted in some 40,000 tins. It's even better tuna than we've been able to get before.

Mail Order benefits from products that taste good "time after time after time," Frechette says, which customers want to have on hand as a staple in their homes—an especially important factor during the pandemic.

THE HOLIDAY HEADACHE

As much as customers have been pleased by Mail Order, running the business itself has been a struggle at times for its managing partners. In the first ten years after the website was launched, Mail Order's business consistently grew between 25 to 40 percent per year, thanks to a dogged devotion to audience analysis and target marketing that contrasted with the more casual approach to business across Zingerman's. Email became a significant tool. Anyone who's ordered once from the catalog receives a constant stream of weekly communications, in print and via email, that point out new products and special offers and provide occasional discounts.

Despite its sophistication in communicating with its audience, Mail Order's wildly uneven sales patterns dogged the company. It seemed impossible to level out the shipment schedule so that Mail Order wasn't swamped during the holidays and tapping its foot the rest of the year. Until the 2010s, Mail Order's perennial solution was to throw people at the problem. It hired as many as eight hundred temporary workers to handle the surge in demand. But that caused as many headaches as it solved.

For one thing, there was the quandary of where to put the extra bodies, along with the inventories of additional goods. As a result, holidays at Mail Order were always space constrained. Another company might have leased an extra warehouse, but it made no sense to the managing partners to grow and then shrink when it was no longer needed. Nor could the company reduce the amount of work space allocated to each employee. They needed to have enough room to move around and find the goods that were in each order. By the mid-2000s, as the Mail Order business celebrated its tenth birthday, the holiday disorganization was becoming dire. Mistakes in filling orders became a huge problem, especially with one of its most popular series of gift boxes, called Weekenders.

These are heavily promoted collections of foods that people can eat right out of the box, with no cooking or sandwich assembly required. For the 2020–2021 holiday season, Zingerman's offered a Chanukah Weekender, with an olive oil cake, kosher sea salt caramels, marzipan lollipops, a bag of chocolate coins known as gelt, and two wooden dreidels. Other choices included a Christmas Weekender, Thanksgiving Weekender, Baked Weekender, the Long Weekender, and the Classic Weekender, all featuring Zingerman's products. Because they contain perishable items, including baked goods, they can't be assembled far in advance.

Initially, Mail Order staff tried lining up rows of boxes and inserting the items in order—first the cakes, then the caramels, then the gelt, etc. But if there were dozens to fill, they might lose count, leading to incomplete boxes. With its pledge that customers didn't need to return anything defective, anyone who complained received a replacement box and got to keep the rest of the food. Meanwhile, Zingerman's was stuck absorbing the cost of two boxes, which became much more expensive than a single missed ingredient. Frechette acknowledges that Zingerman's could have limited the number of boxes it shipped, in hopes of reducing mistakes, but "we didn't want to do that," he says.

More space was not the solution. The company moved three times in six years, and relocating was not something anyone wanted to do again. In 2005, help finally arrived from a familiar place: Toyota, where Root, one of the three managing partners, had worked. University of Michigan professor Jeffrey Liker, a Zingerman's customer, and author of *The Toyota Way,* offered to lend Mail Order one of his PhD students, Eduardo

Lander. He wound up spending three years with Mail Order, teaching the staff some of the concepts of lean manufacturing, which Toyota used to reduce waste and to simplify the way it built its cars.

One of the principles of Lean, as it's called in the manufacturing world, is that the people doing the work should come up with solutions to problems, while managers should be coaches who enable them to do their jobs. After Lander left, subsequent groups of employees and Liker's students came to Mail Order and gave staff additional help in understanding the concept of continuous improvement, or *kaizen* in Japanese, and Mail Order was able to right itself. Those Weekenders strewn all over the company became the centerpiece of a system in which the gift boxes were assembled one at a time. Although that custom construction might take longer than filling items individually, it improved the quality of each box and reduced the need for replacement boxes. The half-filled boxes were no longer strewn everywhere since the next box wasn't started until the one before it was finished.

Condensing the work area also meant that Mail Order didn't have to move again, even though its business doubled during the pandemic, and the company didn't have to bring in as many seasonal employees. Instead of eight hundred per holiday season, it now hires about three hundred extra people for the holidays. Its year-round crew, meanwhile, has grown from fifty to one hundred people. Even though it has smoothed out some of its systems, the holiday crush continues to hover over Mail Order through the year. There's never a moment when it's on the back burner: Once the final gifts are shipped, planning for the following holiday season starts in January. "We spend way too much time and mental resources preparing for every December," Frechette says. "We make every change asking, 'Will this survive in December?'"

Part of the problem, he believes, is that Mail Order staff members have much more experience with nonholiday production than the hectic pace of the winter season. "Even myself, I've only had twenty-six holiday seasons. I've only done it twenty-six times," says Frechette. "The daily things, we get good at. The holiday things, we don't get great at." No other time of the year echoes what Mail Order experiences over the holidays, so there isn't a way for staff to practice what they'll face. "You can't 'make' a holiday," he says. "You think about corporate gifts in America, and when is the only time you get a gift?" The holidays.

As much as Mail Order's partners agonize over their challenges, other parts of Zingerman's see it as an enormous asset. Mangigian says the Lean learnings at Mail Order have helped him in reorganizing the Coffee and Candy companies. The customer feedback that Mail Order receives is shared across Zingerman's, so that each business can get tips and suggestions for how they can improve. And the catalog keeps Zingerman's in touch with University of Michigan alumni, and all the other people who flow in and out of the city. "Ann Arbor is a transient town, but this helps sustain Zingerman's in slow times," Wallag-Muno says.

Most of all, the catalog's success is the result of hard work, thought, and analytics, says Frechette. "As interesting as the catalog is, and the way it represents the look and feel of what we sell, behind it sits spreadsheets and math. That's what drives businesses like ours. It's not glamorous." But it is Zingerman's connection to its community—and those who might like to be part of it.

CHAPTER EIGHT

The Bakehouse

Across the United States, America abounds with great bakeries. Shops in almost every state are turning out crusty, chewy artisanal loaves in endless varieties. Even supermarkets claim that their fresh bread is baked in-house (usually from frozen dough). Instagram teems with pastry chefs displaying their croissants and babka, and baking became a refuge for millions of people stuck at home during the pandemic.

But the baking world was still evolving in 1992 when Zingerman's founded its first significant business beyond the Deli: Zingerman's Bakehouse. From the beginning, Weinzweig and Saginaw knew that good bread was key to the kind of sandwiches they wanted to sell, thanks to the tutelage of meat man Sy Ginsberg. And after ten years of relying on a bakery in suburban Detroit, where they were required to fetch bread themselves, they vowed to begin baking their own.

Weinzweig and Saginaw asked Frank Carollo if he would join them in opening a bakery. Carollo, you may recall, was a partner in Mike Monahan's fish business, who also became one of the Deli's first employees. After seven years working with Monahan, Carollo went to see Weinzweig on his last day at the fish shop and asked Weinzweig whether he had any projects that Carollo could try next. Six months later, Carollo was feeding the sourdough starter that led to the first loaves produced at Zingerman's Bakehouse. The venture started out with only one customer, the Deli, and it planned to focus on six bread recipes.

Thirty years later, the Bakehouse is one of the biggest ventures under the Zingerman's umbrella, and a leading example of the interaction between the ZCoB companies. Bakehouse products are featured at the Deli and the Roadhouse. It provides the toast for the menu at Zingerman's Coffee, and it sends loaves to Zingerman's Catering. It is also an undisputed star of Zingerman's Mail Order. Through Zingerman's bread, cookies, and pastries, people across the country learn about Zingerman's, whether from congratulatory gift baskets, sandwich kits, or just the loaves they order on their own. When things looked darkest during the pandemic, the Bakehouse was a shining star. So many people wanted bread, via Mail Order and from other retail outlets, that the Bakehouse got through the early months of the coronavirus crisis with only a minimal revenue decline for that fiscal year, even though the Deli saw a steep drop in business.

From the beginning, the Bakehouse founders vowed that the enterprise would use locally sourced ingredients, including wheat, rye, and corn flour, and Michigan grains like spelt and einkorn. In the past few years, the Bakehouse joined a growing trend among bread bakers across America and began to mill its own flour (which can be purchased in its retail store, the Bakeshop). All that lay in the future when Carollo brought together his first group of eight employees, which included his future Bakehouse partner, Amy Emberling.

While Carollo grew up in the Detroit suburbs, Emberling is Canadian, a native of scenic Cape Breton Island in Nova Scotia. She grew up in a Jewish family, eating dishes like those served at Zingerman's—brisket, rye bread, matzo ball soup, and pickled herring. She went to Harvard, and then moved to Ann Arbor with the man she eventually married.

Upon arriving, Emberling worked in several restaurant kitchens, left for Paris for a short time to study cooking and baking at the famed cooking school at the Hotel Ritz, and then came back to Ann Arbor. She approached Weinzweig to brainstorm job possibilities. He suggested that she try to get a job with Carollo. The interview took place in the yet-to-open Bakehouse, at a folding card table in the middle of the empty bakery floor. After several days, Emberling didn't have an answer from Carollo and called him to see what was going on. He said he feared she wouldn't be able to support her graduate student husband and young son on the low wage he could offer her. "Isn't it my decision about whether the pay is enough?" Emberling shot back. It was, as the line from *Casablanca* goes, the beginning of a beautiful (if sometimes argumentative) friendship.

As the first business beyond the Deli, the Bakehouse decided that it needed its own mission statement. As Emberling wrote in *Zingerman's Bakehouse*, a book that shares the company's stories and recipes, the original group brainstormed, and came up with a simple motto. "At Zingerman's Bakehouse, we are **passionately** committed to the **relentless pursuit** of being the **best bakery we can imagine**."

The bold-faced words are on purpose, because they won the most staff votes. *Passionately* reflected what was and is an intense work environment. People are on their feet for their entire shifts. They're constantly moving baking trays, wheeling racks, kneading dough, lugging plastic tubs of risen dough, and sliding loaves into the ovens. Emberling says staff surveys sometimes come back saying that the work environment is "not for everyone," but she doesn't want a place that tolerates apathy and low engagement.

The same Toyota-style concepts that Mail Order embraced also influenced the way the Bakehouse is run. The *relentless pursuit* reflects Carollo's passion about his work, which fits the Japanese concept of *kaizen*, one of the Total Quality Management principles taught by W. Edwards Deming. *Best bakery* means not settling for good when great is possible. *We can imagine* is a nod to Zingerman's embrace of Visioning. The Bakehouse isn't market driven, although it regularly introduces new products that fit industry trends.

For instance, in 2018, I noticed that tahini was breaking out of Middle Eastern cuisine. One of the places I saw that happen was in the tahini cookies introduced by the Bakehouse. As with everything that Zingerman's tries to do, Emberling says the Bakehouse is meant to be a place that's purpose and vision driven. Shifting away from peanut butter and to tahini instead allowed the Bakehouse to eliminate peanuts from its products, which many customers avoided due to allergies. "We create a bakery that we imagine is great—the food, the work environment, customer experience, and community engagement," she says. "We try not to be limited to the generally accepted beliefs about how things can be."

THE LEADERSHIP OF FRANKENAMY

Frank Carollo and Amy Emberling dubbed themselves "the optimizer" and "the innovator," respectively. Carollo was focused on details, while Emberling tended to be a big-picture thinker. Just as Saginaw and Weinzweig had become "Paul and Ari" across ZCoB, now the baking pair became "Frank and Amy"—or as their staff put it, "Frankenamy." To the staff, they tried to present a united front, focusing on their similarities. For instance, both loved baking and eating bread, and interacting with staff and customers. It was common to see one or both of them in their T-shirts and baking aprons jumping in at the front counter or helping at the baking tables.

They created a bakery with high standards, in line with those of the country's best bakeries. Many of Zingerman's breads take eighteen to twenty-eight hours to produce, a process that includes steps such as mixing dough, shaping the bread, the time needed for it to rise (called "proofing"), preparing the loaf for its bake, and time spent in the oven. Although some specialty bakeries can take even longer, as many as forty hours for certain types of bread, this mirrors the time that many of the country's best bakers require, and many hours more than a commercial bakery would spend producing its loaves. There are no preservatives, artificial flavorings, or peanuts, although some specialty breads contain walnuts or pecans. While customers can pay ten dollars or more for specialty loaves, like the pecan raisin bread that's my ninety-four-year-old aunt's favorite breakfast, there is a monthly bread special that usually costs six dollars or less. All of it is handmade. The bread bakers stand at large wooden tables, safely socially distanced and wearing masks, kneading, cutting, and preparing loaves that will rise, and then eventually will go into the Bakehouse's commercial ovens.

Some of the bakers attended prestigious culinary schools, such as the Culinary Institute of America, which uses the Bakehouse as one of the outlets in its extern program, or the well-regarded culinary department at Schoolcraft Community College about thirty minutes away. Others are University of Michigan graduates in unrelated fields who were attracted to the baking life. Still more are local kids who decided to apply for the holidays and were subsequently hired full-time.

On an ordinary day, the 150 Bakehouse employees turn out about twelve thousand items. During the holidays, the Bakehouse produces an average of twenty-five thousand items a day. A peak day is thirty-five thousand loaves of bread, cookies, cakes, pastries, and savory things like pretzels. The Bakehouse is divided into several areas. One section at the east end of the building is used by pastry and cookie makers. They work in the evening so that the items they make can be sent the next morning to Mail Order, Zingerman's wholesale customers, and put out for sale in the retail Bakeshop, at the Deli and in the Roadshow, the drive-up food truck outside the Roadhouse. Pastries have a short shelf life, compared with bread, and since they do not contain preservatives, Zingerman's wants them to be as fresh as possible. Between the pastry kitchen and the main baking department sits a shipping area, where loaves, pastries, and other items are sorted into flat plastic bins, labeled according to the customer, and then loaded into trucks and vans.

The cake decorating studio sits on the north side of the building. The cakes are baked by the pastry department, and then are brought into the studio on racks to be iced and decorated. Some of the cakes will be put on sale in the Bakeshop; others are sold whole and in slices at Zingerman's Next Door. The Roadhouse is another customer, as are area cafés. The cake studio houses a specialty crew, skilled in all manner of designs. These decorators can prepare everything from wedding cakes to graduation cakes. Customers can pick out standard designs on a tablet that has dozens of ideas, or they can bring in their own concept.

The decorators can mold figurines out of fondant, and design delicate Japanese cherry blossoms out of gum paste, an edible alternative to sugar. Thanks to the visibility that cake design has received on social media and from food TV shows, these positions have been among the most popular jobs in the Bakehouse. At times, there has been a years-long wait to shift from the Bakehouse into the studio. But for bread lovers like Emberling and Carollo, the most intense action is taking place out on the main production floor.

CONCOCTING A COFFEE CAKE

Anyone who has peeked into the back room at a commercial bakery might be astonished at how much activity is taking place. The Bakehouse is no different. One table is solely devoted to coffee cakes. It is ringed by tall standing ovens, with doors that open like those on a refrigerator. The cakes are assembled in sturdy round fluted Bundt pans, far more durable than one you might use at home. Since the cakes will be turned out onto their bottoms after they are baked, the ingredients are first added to the fluted top.

A sour cream coffee cake begins with a generous dollop of batter, about one-third of the total amount. Then comes a filling that includes toasted walnuts, brown sugar, and cinnamon. Another dollop of batter follows, as does more filling, and then the coffee cake is topped off with the final third of batter and weighed. About five large coffee cakes can fit onto a heavy-duty baking tray, that then slides into a rack. Once the rack is filled with trays, a baker wheels it over to one of the commercial ovens, unlocks the door, slides in the rack, locks the door, and sets the timer.

The baking process is repeated for other types of Zingerman's coffee cakes, like hot cocoa, whose development required the baking crew to test about fifty different recipes before settling on one that actually tasted close to drinking a cup of hot chocolate. Zingerman's sells some unique coffee cake varieties, like New Deli Crumb Cake, a twist on the crumb cakes that have always been popular in East Coast households. New Deli (yes, the play on words is deliberate) is topped with a butter and sugar topping that also includes cardamom, ginger, cloves, coconut, and pistachios. The spices come from Épices de Cru, the Montreal spice merchant.

Just as at the Deli, you'll find fun names scattered around the Bakehouse. Some are self-descriptive, like Big O cookies, its generous version of an oatmeal cookie, Ginger Jump-Up cookies, Just Rhubarb Rhubarb Pie (no strawberries invade the filling), and Better Than San Francisco Sourdough bread. But: What is Hunka Burnin' Love Chocolate Cake? How about Magic Brownies (which appeared on the menu long before 2018, when edibles became legal for consumption in Michigan)?

The first version of Hunka Burnin' Love was created in the late 1980s at the Deli. It's a four-layer, nine-inch round cake that weighs seven pounds—explaining the Hunka part—and can easily satisfy thirty people. It's a fudgy cake, moistened with buttermilk, and topped with a chocolate buttercream icing that has chopped chocolate, egg whites, and sea salt. Magic brownies are essentially brownies with walnut pieces, but when they first appeared at the Deli, each brownie weighed a quarter pound. They were baked in full-sized commercial baking pans, the kind in which office party cakes are made. But the ends often got too crispy, so they were cut off. Emberling, who doesn't like waste, switched the baking process to smaller conventional baking pans, closer to those used in home ovens, so that the brownies did not require trimming. They are part of a brownie lineup that also includes Buenos Aires brownies, filled with dulce de leche, and Townie brownies, a wheat-free version that was created long before many diners were eliminating gluten from their diets.

AN AUSPICIOUS FAILURE

Sometimes products don't catch on, but rather than discontinue them, the Bakehouse will often say they are "on vacation." Examples include 2 kilogram (4.4 pound) loaves of rye bread, and bigger loaves in general. Increasingly, buyers want smaller loaves, that they can eat in a few days and won't go stale, even though the bakers think the larger ones taste better.

The biggest mistake that the Bakehouse ever made, however, was a joint venture with Borders Books & Music, founded by Ann Arbor resident Tom Borders. At its peak, Borders had five hundred stores around the country, including three large ones in Ann Arbor. In 2008, Emberling was approached by a local author and mother of a Roadhouse staffer who had written a book called *The Christmas Cookie Club*.

At the time, the economy was awful (Detroit's carmakers were in Washington, seeking congressional aid) and the Bakehouse was looking for products that could rescue a disappointing season. Emberling convinced Borders to buy 7,000 boxes of its Christmas cookies, requiring the Bakehouse to turn out 150,000 cookies that matched the types mentioned in the book. Four days a week, for three weeks, Emberling and company would come in at 4 a.m. to crank out the Borders cookies.

They packed and shipped twelve boxes off to every Borders store in the United States and Puerto Rico, confident the book and the cookies would be a hit, and waited for a response. There wasn't one. According to Borders sales reports, not a single box of cookies sold before Christmas. The bookstore chain offered a compromise: If Zingerman's was willing to let them sit until January 1, Borders offered to pay for half the cost.

Instead, Emberling asked for all the cookie boxes to be returned. The cookies were deteriorating, and if somebody actually bought some, they might wind up with a crumbled, stale product that would reflect poorly on Zingerman's reputation. The cookies came back from Borders stores, and Emberling disposed of them. "It was too painful and nothing we could do anything about," Emberling says. (Postscript: The Bakehouse now sells its own collections of Christmas cookies, and in 2020, it even created a baking kit so that home bakers could make cookies from its own recipes.)

UNUSUAL DELIGHTS

The Christmas cookie debacle might have made another bakery hesitant to try a bold approach. But when you visit the Bakehouse, you may notice that the lineup includes a number of Hungarian pastries, such as *rétes*, a strudel that can be either savory or sweet, *Esterházy torta*, a walnut cream cake, and *rigó jancsi*, a chocolate cream cake. These types of pastries may be a mystery to most consumers.

How did they get to the Bakehouse? For a fairly simple reason. Emberling and Carollo became fascinated with Hungarian foodways, even though neither of them is Hungarian. Due to its proximity to, and historic relationship with, Austria, Hungarian food became familiar to Central Europeans, often served in cafés in Vienna. The cuisine was especially important in the Hungarian Jewish community, which was decimated in the final months of World War II, and subsequently suppressed during the Cold War.

There was a sizable Hungarian population in New York City, centered in the Upper East Side neighborhood called Yorkville, and in the 1990s, there was a resurgence of interest in Hungarian cooking. Emberling and Carollo traveled to Hungary multiple times, sampling pastries, breads, and other dishes they thought might fit the Bakehouse menu. As it turns out, there is also a Hungarian community in the Detroit area, attracted to the region by the same automotive jobs that lured immigrants from other countries to Michigan.

Emberling says the customers' reactions to the Bakehouse's Hungarian specialties has been overwhelmingly positive, whether from people who have never tried them or from others for whom they bring back memories. As she wrote in the Bakehouse book, "Frank and I love food, but we also love people. This project has been an incredible combination of both, enabling us to make meaningful connections with many people, in new ways and across different worlds. The power to bring people together is remarkable."

CHAPTER NINE

Coffee and Candy and Cheese

Just as Saginaw and Weinzweig hoped, the creation of the Community of Businesses sparked innovation among the Zingerman's staff and led to the creation of its own cottage industries. After the successful launch of the Bakehouse and Mail Order in the 1990s, Zingerman's followed in the 2000s by creating businesses to sell coffee, candy, and dairy-based products like cheese and gelato. In each case, the company was the brainchild of someone who was passionate about those types of products. Because they wrote an appealing vision, Saginaw and Weinzweig were willing to contribute capital so that they could launch their businesses. The trio of food businesses all fit trends of the times when they were started. But despite the desire of the two founders to see these businesses get off the ground, they've all required overhauls and additional investments through the years, and each is now led by someone other than the person who started that business.

ZINGERMAN'S COFFEE

Allen Leibowitz can talk about coffee all day—or all evening, in the case of a classroom full of coffee lovers. In the late 2000s, I was a student at a class he taught upstairs at Zingerman's Next Door about espresso. I arrived hoping to learn how to purchase the right grind for a little espresso machine that I'd received as a gift, and to gain confidence in crafting the perfect drink. Instead, I got more background and history than I could have imagined.

Leibowitz gave us a ninety-minute PowerPoint lecture about coffee, coffee origins, and the theory of coffee preparation before we took our first sip. Then we knocked back about eight espressos in the remaining thirty minutes, and I didn't get to sleep until 4 a.m. But I can still recite the importance of freshly ground coffee beans and the right temperature of water, even though my little espresso machine has long since died.

Leibowitz got hooked on coffee when he worked at Digital Equipment Company in Palo Alto, California. Unlike the fine brews he made for our class, he drank "a dodgy little espresso" that prompted him to explore better Italian roasts, and then to explore single-origin coffees from around the world. When he moved to Ann Arbor, his enthusiasm for coffee led him to seek a meeting in 2000 with Weinzweig and Saginaw where he proposed the creation of Zingerman's Coffee Company. Saginaw and Weinzweig liked the passion he showed for the idea, he says, but felt it was important for Leibowitz to work in Zingerman's businesses to understand how the company worked. So, he first took a job behind the counter at Next Door, selling pastries and beverages, and then joined the crew that was preparing to open the Roadhouse. Once the latter was up and running, Zingerman's Coffee was next, in 2003.

The coffee business made sense at the time. Not only were Ann Arbor residents enthusiastic about coffee, Zingerman's was actually late to the specialty coffee business. Peet's Coffee launched its first shop in 1966, Starbucks was founded in 1971 at the Pike Place Market in Seattle. Blue Bottle, the cult favorite now owned by Nestlé, got on its feet in 2002. In Ann Arbor, Espresso Royale, the city's dominant name in coffee, opened its first local store in 1988, a year after it was started in Oklahoma, and for years was Zingerman's primary local competition. (Espresso Royale's Ann Arbor shops closed in 2020, another victim of the pandemic, although some have been revived as independent businesses.)

Leibowitz knew that backing from Zingerman's could get a fledgling coffeemaker off to a good start. "The Deli alone would be a phenomenal account for any small roaster," Leibowitz says. He began with two coffee roasting machines, which he installed at Mail Order, and started with a coffee blend that could be served by the Roadhouse. In the first year, Leibowitz estimates that Zingerman's Coffee did about $80,000 in business. By 2008, Zingerman's Coffee was logging about $250,000 a year in business, but it came mainly through Zingerman's itself. The coffee company wasn't tapping as completely as it might have into America's swelling enthusiasm for espresso, single-origin coffees, and flavorful blends.

Saginaw was convinced that the coffee company could grow and generate more income. While Leibowitz was a knowledgeable coffee enthusiast, Saginaw felt he needed help on the business side of the operation. In 2007, Ramsey Bishar, co-owner of Big George's, Ann Arbor's most prominent electronics retailer, introduced Saginaw to his friend Steve Mangigian, who had held a series of executive jobs at other companies. While Mangigian didn't have a culinary background, he had an MBA, and his friends were impressed by the way Zingerman's did business. "All of my colleagues said, 'Wouldn't it be great to work at Zingerman's?'" he recalls. "It was just the talk of the town."

Saginaw invited him to attend a partners' meeting, which he enjoyed, but at that time, there did not seem to be the right fit for someone with his extensive business background. Nothing came of the initial courtship. But in 2008, with the economy faltering, and feeling that Coffee was missing out on potential growth, Saginaw asked whether Mangigian might consider joining Zingerman's as a copartner in the coffee company. He felt that Mangigian might have ideas to help the coffee company increase its sales. Now, since a stake in the business was involved, Mangigian thought the arrangement might work. At Zingerman's, "You've got groups of people who are utterly committed to the food, but as a result are not enormous businesspeople," Mangigian says. "They've got great ideas, but don't know how to scale them and don't know how to make them business worthy." While the opportunity interested him, there was one problem: He wasn't a coffee drinker. And before the deal could be finalized, he had to get Weinzweig's approval. He arrived for the meeting to find Weinzweig sitting with eight cups of coffee in front of him. Weinzweig, who was actually a tea drinker, wanted to gauge Mangigian's instincts. Mangigian suspects that Weinzweig had been tipped off that his prospective employee wasn't a coffee lover. "I knew this was the test of all tests," Mangigian says. "Ari intimidated the hell out of me. At that moment, I sipped my first cup of coffee. I tried a few of them. And I passed the Ari test."

CHANGING COFFEE'S APPROACH

While he didn't drink the beverage regularly then (he does now), Mangigian had formed some impressions of the coffee market. "I always felt that in the U.S., coffee was something of a pretentious experience," Mangigian says. Baristas "would want to sell me a highfalutin drink that I don't know anything about." Diving into his research, Mangigian began a series of trips to coffee-producing countries around the world, traveling extensively across Central and Latin America, echoing the kind of research that Weinzweig and other Zingerman's partners frequently did themselves. In El Salvador, he saw that there was "a tremendous disparity between what was going on at origin and what was happening in the U.S. Coffee is the humblest beverage on the planet, and these producers were trying to eke out a meager living." He vowed that Zingerman's would move beyond its blends into more coffees from individual producers, to help these coffee entrepreneurs grow their businesses.

As Mangigian worked alongside Leibowitz for several years, the business began to grow, although the recession kept a damper on its expansion. After a lengthy discussion of an exit plan, Saginaw says he and Leibowitz agreed that it was time to give Mangigian sole charge of the business, which happened in 2012. Leibowitz moved to Houston to be near family, but coffee remained his focus. Since leaving Zingerman's, he has since run a coffee bar, launched a specialty coffee company with his wife, and owns a company that repairs coffeehouse equipment. Once Leibowitz left, Mangigian and Saginaw crafted a plan for accelerating Coffee's growth. Mangigian felt it was time for the business to come down to earth. "I wanted coffee to be approachable and accessible. I didn't want customers coming into our little café and being treated like a dumb ass" as he felt they were at other coffeehouses.

As part of that philosophy, Mangigian wanted Zingerman's to push more deeply into selling its coffee to grocery stores, such as Busch's and Plum Market in southeast Michigan, and the high-volume Meijer's chain, which has about 250 stores across the Midwest. He wanted to offer brewed samples of different coffees to shoppers so they could say, "Wow, that's really different from what I've been drinking."

Soon it became normal to encounter a Zingerman's product demonstrator in the aisles of a grocery store, and to spend a few moments sipping a free sample of the latest coffee variety. Along with a full lineup of espresso and other drinks available at Next Door, Zingerman's also opened its own coffeehouse at Zingerman's South, where patrons could order their favorite hot or iced coffee drinks (including a powerful cold brew), as well as pastries and toasts topped with Zingerman's cheeses and other ingredients. There was a classroom where students could learn about Zingerman's different brews, and customers could get tours of the operation. The coffeehouse kept a bare-bones industrial look, and prior to the pandemic, became a favorite work space and gathering space for locals.

Says Mangigian, "Coffee is for everybody. Why should we make great food available only to the elite? I had a real conviction that this was the way forward." Along with grocery stores, Zingerman's Coffee focused on independent cafés, but he found them a harder sell than the supermarkets. "With a grocery store, you go in and say, would you like to buy our coffee?" and the manager might order thirty cartons. "A café requires a lot of care. But the money is in the cafés," since grocers often discount coffee products, and Zingerman's blends would be stacked next to those of other producers.

Mangigian was especially pleased when Zingerman's Coffee became available at the café inside the Ross School of Business at Michigan, the first of a series of colleges where he won business. Then Zingerman's landed a major score—at least, for the mid-2010s. It secured a contract with HBF Paradies, the airport retailer, giving it the opportunity to sell coffee at airports in Atlanta, San Francisco, Salt Lake City, Washington, DC, as well as Detroit, where it partnered with Plum Market. By 2019, Zingerman's Coffee had grown to annual revenue of about $4.8 million, or twenty times the amount it sold in its first year. Pleased by Coffee's transformation, Saginaw tapped Mangigian for help in another lagging part of ZCoB.

ZINGERMAN'S CANDY

In the early 2010s, Saginaw and Mangigian took a business trip to New York City. They made a sales call to Shake Shack, the burger business launched by restaurateur Danny Meyer. "We wanted to sell them candy bars," Mangigian recalled, "and Paul said, 'You're the guy who knows how to make deals.'"

It was another business that had never been a passion with Mangigian. "I had no interest in candy, whatsoever." But, after the trip, Saginaw suggested that Mangigian create the same kind of jump start for the candy business that he had given to the coffee company.

Zingerman's Candy was founded in 2009 by someone who did love chocolate—Charlie Frank, who began working at the Bakehouse in 2001. He trained at the Culinary Institute of America and had worked as a pastry chef at numerous places. The jobs allowed him to delve into his love of sugar work, indulging a lifelong passion. As a young boy, he would spend fifty cents a week on sweets when he was walking home from piano lessons. He would pick out enough penny candy to last him for a week, until his next lesson. Frank joined Zingerman's with the intent of creating and launching his own business. A year into his position as manager of the pastry department, Frank came up with an idea for candy bars, and he began working on a vision for a candy company.

He called his candy bar line Zzang! Bars, and developed five varieties which he made in a corner of Mail Order's operations. They included the original Zzang! Bar, with layers of caramel, peanut butter, nougat, and roasted peanuts, enrobed in dark chocolate. The Cashew Cow Bar had cashew brittle, cashews, and milk chocolate gianduja (a sweet chocolate hazelnut spread) covered in dark chocolate. There was also the Peanut Butter Crush Bar, with crunchy rice and peanut butter; Wowza, which had raspberry chocolate ganache, jellied raspberries, and raspberry nougat; and What the Fudge?, with fudge, caramel, and malted milk cream fondant.

The candy bars were individually packaged in colorful yellow boxes and sold at the Deli and a few retail outlets. But they were a little too big to eat at one sitting, and were also pricey, compared with ordinary candy bars, retailing at about four dollars each. Frank was "a sugar genius," Mangigian says, but the candy company remained "a small cottage industry, selling to a handful of customers inside and a few outside." Frank, he says, made candy bars that he liked, not necessarily those that found a wide audience. In 2014, the candy business was struggling, with revenue of only about $300,000 annually, and was not returning the investment Zingerman's had made in it.

As part of the overhaul, Saginaw suggested that Mangigian take a stake in the business. "I said, 'I'm happy to help out, I'm happy in coffee, I don't need a piece of the action,'" he replied. Saginaw insisted, and Mangigian wound up buying about a third of the candy business. But Frank would remain the managing partner, while Candy's marketing team looked for ways to pump up its visibility. They got some help from Oprah Winfrey. In 2008, Gayle King traveled the country tasting sandwiches for an article in *Esquire*, and introduced Winfrey to Zingerman's. Winfrey then put the Deli's brisket sandwich on her list of Favorite Things and treated her television audience to samples during a show that November.

Winfrey subsequently discovered Zzang! Bars and put them on her Favorite Things list in 2011. In 2014, the candy bars were included in gift bags for Academy Award nominees, while Winfrey also named its peanut brittle as one of her O! List picks. According to Mangigian, the attention from Oprah didn't lead to a sales boom. But the endorsements did draw attention to the products, which went on sale alongside other Zingerman's items at the Plum Market in Detroit's airport and in Plum Market grocery stores.

With Candy sales improving, in 2017, Zingerman's opened the Zingerman's Candy Manufactory store in Zingerman's South, where it sold candy bars, peanut brittle, spiced peanuts, and seasonal candy. Soon after, however, Frank learned his parents were ill, and decided to sell his shares of the candy company. In 2018, Mangigian became the managing partner for both Candy and Coffee, a rarity in ZCoB, but a workable solution given Candy's smaller size. By 2019, it was achieving annual revenue of about $750,000, based on growth of about 8 to 10 percent a year. That's only a fraction of the multimillion-dollar revenue of the Deli and the Bakehouse, let alone the massive appeal of Mail Order.

While Candy has some devoted fans, the group is admittedly small.

"I'm not beating my chest about it," Mangigian says about the financial performance. "It's a stepchild." But he is convinced the business has potential. "I'm not a quitter," Mangigian says. "I'm going to go so far as saying that Candy is going to be a shining star."

Plum Market has given Zingerman's feedback on ways that its candy can appeal to more customers, and it has given prime shelf space to Zingerman's products next to its checkout lanes. Candy has recently introduced new variations on its chocolate bars, including snack sizes. "We're going to level out our cost structure," Mangigian says, "and produce what we need to produce."

ZINGERMAN'S CREAMERY

In a deli anywhere, one menu item you're bound to find is a bagel with cream cheese. In the streets of New York, they're sold from coffee carts. You can find pre-assembled ones in a refrigerator case at Zabar's, and in practically any bagel shop, you can pick up a tub of cream cheese in a variety of flavors. The Deli was no different, but for the first eighteen years it was in business, it used commercial cream cheese. Although it tried to buy the best version of someone else's cream cheese that it could find, there was a feeling that it could do better, especially since artisanal cream cheeses had started to appear in specialty stores.

There was another need for a good cream cheese: The Bakehouse wanted a superior product as an ingredient in its baked goods, too. In 2001, John Loomis, Dave Carson, Weinzweig, and Saginaw combined forces to launch Zingerman's Creamery, the fifth business in ZCoB, with Loomis serving as the managing partner. It began by making one product: Real Cream Cheese (on which Zingerman's holds a trademark).

Unlike Philadelphia brand or another commercial cheese, Zingerman's cream cheese is more like a spreadable French cheese, with tangy and salty overtones. A little goes a long way. Zingerman's sells individual portions at the Bakehouse that look like they will barely cover half of a bagel, at least compared with the schmears that other delis and New York City coffee carts slather onto their bagels. But that small amount packs a lot of flavor.

The location of the Creamery was distinctly different from the other ZCoB businesses. Loomis set up a production facility in Manchester, Michigan, a rural town about twenty-five minutes from Ann Arbor. To produce the cream cheese, Zingerman's takes fresh milk from the Calder Family Dairy, a local company, pasteurizes it, and then pours it into a vat where rennet and active cultures are added. After a few hours, it forms a curd. This is hand-cut with steel knives, then hung in cloth bags for the excess moisture to drain off. Once it's drained, sea salt and cream are added to the curd, and the mixture is carefully blended. There's none of the vegetable gum or preservatives that you'll find in a tub of Philadelphia, and that means it needs to be eaten or used within days of buying it.

The Creamery also began to explore other products that it could produce, and the Roadhouse served as its source of inspiration. When the Roadhouse opened, one of its most popular appetizers became pimiento cheese, a tangy spread with a recipe discovered by Weinzweig that's a combination of cheddar, black pepper, cayenne, and of course, pimientos. While it's a staple across the South, pimiento cheese was something of a mystery for many Midwesterners when it appeared on the Roadhouse menu, myself included, but I loved its creamy texture and the little kick that ended each bite. I introduced numerous Midwestern friends to it, and one year on my birthday, Weinzweig sent me a plate of pimiento cheese, bearing a candle and "Happy Birthday" written on the plate. The Creamery subsequently crafted its own recipe for pimiento cheese that could be packaged and sold to wholesale customers.

Soon the Creamery's lineup began to grow, with an assortment of spreadable and aged cheeses, from cow's and goat milk, eventually reaching a rotating assortment of sixteen different cheeses, in about thirty different varieties. Zingerman's cheeses began to win awards, and the Creamery's own products joined the dozens on sale at the Deli. As the lineup grew, the Creamery needed to open a much larger production facility, which it did in 2003 at Zingerman's South.

A new face also appeared on the Creamery scene. Aubrey Thomason, who started working at the Deli at age seventeen, joined the Creamery in 2007 as a production assistant. Intense in her love for cheese, she educated herself by traveling across Europe. In 2012, at age twenty-six, she joined Loomis as a managing partner, taking over when he retired two years later. Pre-pandemic, the Creamery was buying about 1,500 gallons of cow and goat milks, which it used to make soft cheese such as mozzarella, burrata, and spreadable goat cheese, and aged cheeses from both types of milk.

Along with cheese, Zingerman's branched into a sweeter area: gelato.

Anyone who's traveled to Italy knows the joy of choosing a small cone or a bigger dish with flavors that might have been made that morning. Many cities and college towns have gelaterias, which mimic that travel experience. But gelato was less common in America when Zingerman's began to produce it, not long after it launched the Creamery. As I learned when I took a gelato class at Zingerman's, gelato is much denser than ice cream. The Zingerman's product is essentially milk, Demerara sugar, and a variety of flavors.

The selection of about fifteen flavors changes seasonally, but the basic flavors include strawberry, variations on chocolate including dark chocolate and chocolate hazelnut, vanilla, and sorbets such as raspberry and lemon. (In 2021, Zingerman's had yet to add a plant-based ice cream, although nondairy ice creams had become a fast-growing trend in the frozen dessert world.)

With all those cheeses and frozen treats, by the mid-2010s, the Creamery was outgrowing its space at Zingerman's South, and it also had to make decisions about modernizing in order to comply with federal manufacturing requirements. It was a risky decision. While the Creamery was producing well-received products, it also was one of the highest-cost businesses to run, and was routinely in the red. But it fit the founders' definition of a company with passionate owners, and seemed too essential not to sustain, especially since its cream cheese was a key ingredient at the Deli and the Bakehouse. In 2017, Zingerman's decided to sink $1 million into a renovation that took about nine months and transformed the Creamery into a mini–gourmet store called the Cream Top Shop. It sold Zingerman's cheeses and gelato, as well as other types of cheese, snacks, pantry items, beer, wine, and fresh-made toasted sandwiches. Like Coffee and Candy, the Creamery's products were migrating to grocery stores, who sold prepackaged versions of its cream, goat and pimiento cheese, while pints of gelato could be found in freezer sections of local supermarkets.

Arend Elston, a Chicago businessman, approached Zingerman's about purchasing organic milk from his family's dairy farm in rural Brown City, a couple of hours north of Ann Arbor in an area of Michigan called the Thumb. Elston, who earned an engineering degree from Hope College in western Michigan, scoped out a wealth management career in New York City, where he worked for AllianceBernstein, and eventually in Chicago, where he was a portfolio manager for State Street. Simultaneously, Elston joined his father and his brothers in adding farmland to their property, taking steps so that their products could be certified organic. He had originally approached Plum Market to supply them with some of his family's organic milk, but since the market had its own suppliers, it connected him instead with Zingerman's. After discussions with Saginaw and others, Elston agreed to invest in the Creamery, and then became its owner/operator when Thomason retired early from Zingerman's due to health problems in 2019. "I didn't intend to be on the ground running things, originally," Elston recalls. For a time, he held his Chicago investment position and oversaw the Creamery remotely, with frequent visits to Ann Arbor, but in June 2020 he left his investment job to devote himself full-time to the Creamery.

Elston was in a unique situation, as the only leader of a ZCoB company who was not a managing partner. In 2021, he was still completing the path to partnership. Elston says his main task is to "make sure the Creamery is on good footing for products we want to introduce going forward." He sees the potential to overhaul the gelato lineup and to keep expanding the variety of cheeses. "There will be some changes, for sure," he says. As a newcomer viewing Zingerman's with fresh eyes, Elston is enthusiastic about Zingerman's transparency and its emphasis on top-quality products. "It's a company that leads with food and service first," he says. "A lot of companies lead with finance first."

With the Creamery's sandwiches, the toast offerings at Zingerman's Coffee, and a variety of sandwiches, salads, and soups at the Bakehouse, Zingerman's turned its industrial park into a place to sample their foods. They encouraged customers to take a Tour de Food of all its businesses and marketed a Tour de Food T-shirt. Just before the pandemic, Zingerman's renovated a courtyard next to the Bakehouse to offer outdoor seating, while tables and chairs also were available outside the business for those who wanted to dine alfresco. The open-air plaza was useful when Michigan closed indoor restaurant spaces to fight the spread of COVID-19.

While the casual setting outside the food business was much different than the Deli or the Roadhouse, patrons could enjoy the unique experience of dining within a few feet of the places where their food and drink were manufactured, even if conversations were occasionally interrupted by the sound of small planes coming in for a landing at the nearby airport. And, without traveling elsewhere in Ann Arbor, visitors could get a sense of what Zingerman's had to offer.

CHAPTER TEN

What It's Like to Work at Zingerman's

The cheerfulness and helpfulness of a Zingerman's experience is consistent across its restaurants, food shops, training programs, and special events. You're greeted by the first employee who spots you. Everyone seems to be in a pretty good mood, although you can see that there is lots of activity going on around you. You might not get waited on immediately at the Deli, Next Door, or the Bakeshop, since there are bound to be other customers. But that gives you a chance to browse and think about what you might like to order.

Once you are waited on, it is as if no other customers exist. Whether you're spending hundreds of dollars on a selection of spices, olive oils, and coffee cakes, just ordering a craft beer at the Roadhouse bar, or taking home a loaf of bread for under ten dollars, you get that same patient attention, and "What else can I do for you?" before your order is rung up or your check is presented. For anyone who's trudged through a sprawling supermarket or stood confused before aisles of expensive but mysterious gourmet products, the service you receive at Zingerman's is a revelation—and entirely by design.

But what's it actually like on the inside? Many Zingerman's businesses are places where people went to work and stayed for years, something in common with Ann Arbor itself, where some students like the surroundings so much that they never leave. This group includes Bob Bennett, executive chef at Zingerman's Roadhouse, who went to work at the Deli in 2001. He started at the sandwich line and worked there for about two years, in between his studies at a variety of Michigan colleges, before ending up at Washtenaw Community College, where he ultimately decided to get serious about culinary studies.

"I was never one of those kids who said, 'I'm going to be this,' or 'I'm going to be that,'" Bennett says. At the Deli, "I liked the people I worked with and the high pace of action. It was kind of a gradual building of good things. You just kind of felt accepted, a place where people appreciated what I was doing." Bennett had just started the culinary program at WCC when he heard that Alex Young, with whom he had worked at the Deli, was putting together the original staff at the Roadhouse. The idea of Zingerman's first table-service restaurant was exciting, and Bennett decided to apply, even though he didn't have formal kitchen skills.

In his Roadhouse interview, he was asked whether he knew the classic mother sauces or how to make mashed potatoes. "And I was like, 'I know how to make sandwiches.'" He realized, "I've got some things to learn. Because on top of liking the pace of restaurants, I'm super-ultracompetitive, whatever I want to do. So, I want to be really good at it."

Bennett arrived before Zingerman's finished renovating the mid-century brick building. It had been part of the Bill Knapp's chain of casual eateries, famous across the Midwest for offering diners "a snack or a meal." To occupy his time, he took on many tasks and jotted down notes. One day, he joined other staff in painting the outside walls. He watched kitchen equipment being installed, including the grill that he would be operating. He saw city inspectors go through their checklists, watched Young setting up the process flow for the cooks, until finally, the Roadhouse was ready for its soft opening.

The employees had spent the previous two days getting acquainted with the menu. They expected only friends and family to be on hand to sample the food, allowing them the chance to work out any kinks. But word had spread through the community that the Roadhouse was accepting customers. Instead of the small crowd they anticipated, five hundred people showed up on that first night, eager to see what a formal Zingerman's restaurant would look like. "It was crazy to me," Bennett remembers. The demand did not let up, and his days as a grill chef were long, especially combined with school. "I would start here at two o'clock in the afternoon, work all the way till close, which could be like midnight, one o'clock, and then go to classes at six in the morning," he says.

Many guests expected to be able to order the same sandwiches and side dishes available at the Deli. But Young created a menu that featured "really good American food," from fried chicken and barbecue to macaroni and cheese, accompanied by slices of crusty bread from the Bakehouse. Although some were disappointed that they couldn't simply get a corned beef sandwich, customers and the restaurant community became aware that the Roadhouse was serving well-prepared food, and the restaurant swiftly gained national attention. Beginning in 2007, Young snagged annual nominations from the James Beard Foundation as one of the Best Chefs in America, ultimately winning after his fifth nod in 2011.

Meanwhile, Bennett was learning his craft. Along with building his culinary knowledge, he was accumulating kitchen management skills. But after a few years, he thought he wanted to aim higher. He wanted to "get some more kitchen experience so that I could go to a big city like Chicago," he says. Leaving the Roadhouse, he worked at several Ann Arbor restaurants that have since closed and realized that Zingerman's focus on quality and employee communication had spoiled him.

Rather than move away, Bennett and his wife decided to put down roots in Ann Arbor and start their family. He returned to the Roadhouse, again staffing the grill station, but this time with an eye on advancement.

Bennett began studying how Zingerman's management principles applied in a restaurant setting, especially its philosophy of servant leadership. "It fit with who I was," he says. Unlike some chefs who bark orders at staff, "I'm not really a yeller in the kitchen. I want to be on the front lines with my team, and I feel guilty when I'm not. I think that's right at the core of servant leadership. And that's why it resonates with me pretty well."

CLIMBING THE LADDER

Bennett decided to write a vision for his goal of running the Roadhouse, and approached Young to talk about his ambitions. "I said, 'I really want to be here. Long term, I'd like to be executive chef of this restaurant. [Young] thought about it and said, 'Okay, we can start working toward that.'" Unbeknownst to Bennett, Young was drafting plans to open his own restaurant on the west side of Ann Arbor, a couple of miles from the Roadhouse. "He came to us [in 2017] and said, 'Hey, this is what I'm doing, I'm leaving,'" Bennett says of Young.

As soon as he heard Young was leaving, Bennett immediately got in touch with Saginaw and Weinzweig, and shared his vision, which included the goal of someday replacing Young as the managing partner. Bennett outlined a plan that would stick with the Roadhouse's basic core dishes, but he wanted the menu to have more input from Roadhouse staff. "I'm trying to build more around our team, hearing their ideas and get them learning about food and what presents itself," Bennett says. He also wanted to capitalize on Ann Arbor's farmer's markets, including one that the Roadhouse held in its parking lot every Thursday during the summer, and to source produce from local farmers, including Tammie Gilfoyle of Tamchop Farms, who is Weinzweig's romantic partner, and Melvin Parson, a Black farmer from nearby Ypsilanti who founded the We The People Growers Association to teach others in the area to grow vegetables.

Given the Roadhouse's reputation, Saginaw and Weinzweig under-standably could have sought an award-winning chef with a culinary de-gree from a major city. Instead, Zingerman's decided to promote Bennett to executive chef, sending a signal throughout the organization. "It's a commitment to the staff, a commitment to growing people, and empow-ering them with the freedom to build a vision," Bennett says. "Around every corner, they are looking for input from folks. Every, every time, it was, 'Hey, what do you all think?'"

While he isn't the managing partner—Weinzweig is filling that role—Bennett's Roadhouse kitchen is staffed with many coworkers who have been with Zingerman's for ten years or more. While COVID forced the restaurant to contract, Bennett remains on the lookout for talented hires. Candidates should be interested in excelling at restaurant work and understanding the rigors of a busy kitchen. "We try to promote positiv-ity and build people up and the people who fight really hard against that kind of make it tough to thrive in this atmosphere."

Does Bennett ever wish he'd gone to Chicago or New York or New Orleans? "I don't think so. I still enjoy visiting those places, but I wouldn't change a thing. I'm super excited to be here, and I want to be here as long as I can."

TAKING THE PHILOSOPHY ALONG

People do leave Zingerman's, of course, and it hasn't escaped the depar-tures that took place during the pandemic. There's a long list of staff and business owners throughout the restaurant world who are Zingerman's alumni. Some venture beyond the food field, and become academics, au-thors, and even yarn-store owners. But they take the Zingerman's phi-losophy with them, and apply it to what they do next.

Christine Cook, a professor and doctoral candidate at Wayne State

University in Detroit, worked two stints at the Deli in its early years. Her first job came after she graduated from Princeton University and moved to Ann Arbor in the late 1980s. That lasted about six months, until she went for training in the U.S. military.

When she returned to Ann Arbor, she applied at two places—Borders and Zingerman's. "Borders had a test that you had to take, and I guess I didn't pass," Cook recalls. But along with her earlier stint at the Deli, she had previously worked in a bakery in Harrisburg, Pennsylvania, as well as a winery, and had sufficient retail experience to be rehired at Zingerman's in its grocery section. She and Zingerman's were a good fit. "I kind of was in tune with the concept of the customer is right, treat the customer well, and they had this desire to have people who were always up," Cook says. "I had that attitude. They thought I would jive pretty well." She began at $5.75 an hour, a lower wage than sandwich makers, whose jobs required a higher level of food service skill. For her initiation, Cook had to memorize the names and ingredients of all sixty-two sandwiches on the Deli's sandwich board. She started with the row of turkey sandwiches, then moved on to beef and other categories. Thirty years later, "I could probably tell you twenty of them, complete with the number," Cook says. "There were a few weird ones that nobody ever ordered."

Cook remembers having constant contact with Saginaw, with whom she would frequently discuss the concepts behind Zingerman's Guiding Principles. She saw Weinzweig less often: "He was probably off on some food-tasting adventure in Spain," she says. But Cook says both of the founders would jump in to help when the Deli became slammed with customers, as it often was on football Saturdays. On those days, Cook showed up at 4 a.m. to cut trays of brownies, slice cheesecakes, and otherwise help prepare for the deluge that was about to take place. She enjoyed the hours she spent getting the store ready to welcome customers.

The remaining time, "Oh my God," Cook says. She constantly worried that Zingerman's famous service wouldn't survive a crush of business. "The execution is nearly impossible" when the Line is out the door and around the block, Cook says. "The blood pressure is going up. The smile is plastered to your face." Abra Berens, the chef and cookbook author, arrived at the Deli a few years after Cook, and says she used to fume when she would hear people in the Line griping about the high prices for sandwiches. She'd say to herself, "Well, I'm a part-time person, and I get health insurance." Berens acknowledges that Zingerman's cheerful employees were sometimes derided around Ann Arbor as belonging to a cult, "but if all cults were like Zingerman's, that would be great."

Berens says she worked her way from order taker into a kitchen job at the Deli by constantly peppering Rodger Bowser, one of its managing partners, with questions. "Hey, Rodger, I want to make chicken paprikash," she'd ask, and he would show her. She volunteered to help make the potpies that Zingerman's sells in the winter. Berens spent a day learning to make knishes. Eventually, she was working in the kitchen two days a week, and on the sales floor two days a week. Her eventual transition to cooking came when an employee fell off his bike, and Bowser tapped her to work in the kitchen full-time.

It was far from glamorous. Berens remembers toting hot chicken stock to a full-sized cooler in the summer, and standing with the door open just to cool off. But she saw others around her working just as hard, and observed servant leadership in action. Once, she and Bowser were standing near the Deli's kitchen holding full trays of food, and Bowser spotted a customer who was looking for an empty table. "Rodger said, 'Let me put these down and get that clean for you,'" Berens recalls. "He didn't go over to Next Door and yell at people for not wiping tables down." Deli managing partner Rick Strutz says managers are aware of the pressures that employees face. On a Saturday football weekend in its peak years, "You would have ten thousand guests in a really little space. That little bitty eight-hundred-square-foot deli and the mosh pit of people was amazing to me. It's a real bitch to blow ten thousand minds in a weekend."

GREAT EXPECTATIONS

After forty years, and with a seasoned management philosophy at its fingertips, very little at Zingerman's is left to chance with new employees. As I mentioned in Chapter 5, each receives a checklist, called a "training passport," which lays out a road map for what they will learn. Katie Frank, the managing partner at ZingTrain, shared the checklist that a retail employee at Zingerman's Bakehouse receives when they join the company. This one is typical for those who interact with the public.

The document is divided into timelines for a week, a month, and two months. It lists seven skills that employees are expected to learn in their first seven days on the job, plus a second set of four skills that they need to acquire in their first thirty days, and a third set focusing on two areas to master after sixty days. Everything that the employee needs to know is clearly spelled out. There are plenty of people around, from colleagues to managers to Bakehouse partner Amy Emberling, to reinforce the steps. It's common to see new hires shadowing veteran staff in both the retail area and in the baking preparation area itself, a system that Zingerman's uses throughout its operations.

At some point during that first week, new hires will attend Welcome to the Bakehouse, an orientation session and tour. The new employees walk through every part of the building and hear from one of Zingerman's leaders, often Weinzweig, as well as Emberling. Each employee learns about the history of the company as well as the business where they are working. Then each receives a training packet, which is where they will first encounter the passport, and they are familiarized with Zingerman's training contract. It spells out what the new employee is expected to achieve, and the help that those training them pledge to give. Zingerman's wants to avoid situations where newbies are thrown into the fire with no preparation, which can be common in other types of workplaces.

The retail employee passport is divided into four sections. The first lists the skill that the employee is expected to master—for instance, talking to customers on the telephone, which became even more important during the pandemic. In the second section, the passport lists tasks required to do the job properly, such as greeting a telephone customer politely, knowing how to put them on hold, transferring the call to the appropriate person who can answer their question, checking voice mail if there are messages, and correctly taking a phone order for bread or pastries.

Pffft, you might say, everybody knows how to use a phone. Well, they don't, always. In an era where younger people are constantly using smart phones, the concept of how a business telephone works is not as familiar as it would have been to Generation X or Baby Boomers. Rather than assume that new hires know what to do, the Bakehouse makes sure that they get the instructions they need. That information is also posted on a skill sheet that the employees can refer to, and their knowledge is tested by a manager.

Other skills require hands-on instruction, such as the way to safely operate a bread slicer or how to slice some loaves by hand, the process of opening and closing the shop, keeping storage areas clean, and stocking the shelves and counters promptly with fresh bread and pastries. Within their first week, Bakehouse employees are tested on their product knowledge—both for the items regularly stocked there and special-order items that require twenty-four to forty-eight hours advance notice. In each case, there's a written test to see whether they know what they're selling. While the Bakehouse specializes in bread and goodies, it also has shelves of baking products, cold cases with soups, salads and cheeses, and seasonal items, like cranberry pecan bread in late fall, and kits to bake Christmas cookies.

After that first week, the new employee is bumped up to more sophisticated responsibilities. Now that they know how to open or close the shop, they are expected to complete a checklist for either responsibility by 7 a.m. or 7 p.m. They learn how to place orders for the amount of each product that the Bakehouse expects to sell that day—for instance, the number of loaves of rye bread that will be needed, or how many of the different types of muffins, croissants, and bagels, on a day when bagels are available. They must know how to stock the display cases for all types of foods so that they meet Zingerman's standards. Then there is a second-level test that judges their product acumen.

Sixty days into their job, employees at the Bakehouse are down to the final stretch. They will learn the daily oven schedule for the breads that Zingerman's regularly sells, as well as the specialty breads that are only available once in a while, like pumpernickel raisin or Parmesan bacon. The oven schedule is one of the quirks of the Bakehouse that both delights and irritates some of its customers. In many bakeries, breads come out of the oven all at once, usually in the morning, so that the shelves are fully stocked when the doors open. Once a bread sells out, that's it—there's no more for that day.

But Zingerman's staggers its baking, for a couple of reasons. For one thing, it has multiple customers for its breads beyond people waiting to purchase them. Its internal and wholesale customers need to receive their breads on a fixed schedule. For instance, the Roadhouse gets its bread first thing in the morning so that it can feed its diners, and also provide bread for sale at the Roadshow, the vintage trailer that handles its carryout business. Meanwhile, loaves for grocery-store customers need to be crated and lined up to go onto trucks.

Since it doesn't have the capacity to serve everybody at once, the loaves that are for sale at the Bakehouse come out of the ovens at different times of the day. Those loaves also have to cool off before they can be placed on shelves or sliced. Numerous times throughout the day, Bakehouse employees patiently explain to customers that the bread they're looking for isn't ready yet, but they'd be happy to reserve a loaf for them.

The final steps of the Bakehouse passport include three ZingTrain classes aimed at ramping up their selling skills. They are the Art of Selling

Great Bread and the Art of Selling Great Pastry. Attendance at both earns the employee a ten-dollar gift card. Their final class is Sell Food, Have Fun. Once they've completed that session, they've finished all the items on the passport. And they probably could run their own bakery someday.

Anyone who has worked in retail will be impressed by that level of focus for each employee. When I worked at the now-defunct Jacobson's Department Store, I was taught how to run a cash register, enter a credit-card number, and if I needed to know more, I was told to ask a coworker or a manager. I learned primarily by observation. Executives everywhere will tell you that employee training is an investment, and with pandemic cutbacks and people working from home, training for a time took a backseat to keeping enterprises going. But at Zingerman's, teaching employees is vital to ensuring the consistency of the experience that customers receive. And, it becomes ingrained—even if they don't go on to food careers.

After her second stint at Zingerman's, Christine Cook decided to focus on her writing and teaching career, right around the time that Weinzweig and Saginaw were writing the original vision that resulted in ZCoB. And while she's never returned to retail, she says her Zingerman's experience has guided her approach as a professor. At the start of a semester, she tells her students, "'I'm here to teach you guys. I really want to have you learn what I'm teaching.' I'm willing to try to customize what I do for my teaching to try to appeal to what that person needs at this point. That [approach] kind of probably is left over from my time at Zingerman's," Cook admits.

Her Deli training dies hard. Thanks to the system she learned there, "I will create what my husband will call incantations," Cook says. She tells herself, "'Do this first, and this, and this and this.' I got that from the checklist for opening and closing. Cut the cheesecakes, then oversee the salads. I will know the second anything is beginning to turn bad, foodwise." She laughs. "It helps me if I'm cleaning out my fridge."

Berens, meanwhile, has found that Zingerman's philosophy hasn't permeated the food world as much as she would have hoped. She did find evidence of its practices when she worked at Neal's Yard Dairy's shop in London's Borough Market, which was managed by a Zingerman's alumni. But in subsequent jobs in Chicago, she encountered what she described as culture shock. She recalls thinking, "'What do you mean, you don't care about my opinion? What do you mean, you don't know about servant leadership? What do you mean, there's no Open Book Management?' That constant striving is not common everywhere."

Yet there can be surprises in places you might not think to look. Douglas Botsford grew up in Ann Arbor and worked in a variety of local restaurants, although never at a Zingerman's outpost. He left town for Colorado, where he managed a branch of Jax Fish House & Oyster Bar, a group of popular restaurants near Denver. Unbeknownst to him, owner Dave Query was a friend of Weinzweig's, and had incorporated many of Zingerman's management principles across the restaurants. On his first day there, Botsford recalls, he and other new employees attended an orientation session. One of the managers got up to start a video, then turned to the group. "He asked us, 'Have you heard of this company called Zingerman's?'" Botsford says. He couldn't help laughing as he raised his hand.

Botsford learned Query's interpretation of a number of Zingerman's concepts, such as Visioning and Open Book Management. Jax also offered health care for its employees as well as profit sharing. "It was great," Botsford says of his experience there. With that introduction to Zingerman's concepts under his belt, he returned to Ann Arbor, where he and a longtime friend and local chef, Sean Morin, became partners in an oyster and seafood focused food truck called Juicy Oistre. They joined a vibrant group of young cooks taking part in driveway events and pop-ups hosted by local food businesses, where they sold everything from Cuban sandwiches and bento boxes to dumplings and handcrafted pastries.

One night, Botsford and Morin revved up their grills at an Ann

Arbor gourmet shop called York, whose long outdoor yard had become a popular gathering spot for people from the area. As dozens of millennials and other food lovers waited patiently to try their menu, a tall man stood off to the side, watching. It was Weinzweig. A few weeks later, there was a pop-up outside Zingerman's Creamery, featuring a local cook, Gregorio DiMarco, who calls himself Chef G. DiMarco's menu—porchetta panino, smoked cauliflower Reuben, and a Cubano sandwich—incorporated Creamery products, such as mozzarella and goat cheese, and were prepared on Bakehouse bread, accompanied by his own paprika potato chips. As customers lined up to buy his sandwiches and eat them at nearby tables, it was clear that Zingerman's principles and new cooking philosophies could happily coexist.

PART FOUR

Beyond Ann Arbor

Zingerman's Roadshow serves customers from a drive-up trailer outside
Zingerman's Roadhouse. (Photograph by Maalek Getchell)

CHAPTER ELEVEN

Teaching Others

It was a balmy Monday evening in New Orleans, and I was looking forward to a tasty meal at Atchafalaya Restaurant, a small, hip restaurant just off Magazine Street in the Uptown neighborhood. Joined by public radio broadcaster Tess Vigeland, I settled into one of the tables, glanced across the room, and did a double take. There, accompanied by three guests, sat Ella Brennan, the matriarch of one of the city's best-known restaurant families, and the owner of Commander's Palace, one of its most heralded places. Ti Martin, Miss Ella's daughter, says that investigatory dinner was typical of her mother. "Even when she was ninety-one, she was still trying to get it better," she says.

The restaurant world can be both a collegial and competitive place. Chefs and restaurant owners are constantly watching like hawks to see how others are doing business, and admittedly borrowing ideas whenever they can. But the approach at Zingerman's is different. Before the pandemic, it had built a $2 million business, ZingTrain, based on sharing its staff-friendly operating philosophies, in hopes of feeding other companies' bottom-line success. Restaurants need help anywhere they can find it. In recent years, food establishments have faced two types of pressures. One was the harsh spotlight the #MeToo movement shone on abusive chefs and proprietors, like Mario Batali, a longtime Zingerman's admirer whose career crumbled after he was accused of sexual harassment, and John Besh, who pretty much disappeared from the New Orleans scene amid allegations that he mistreated female employees.

At the same time, economic pressures have never been heavier. Even before the pandemic, owners were desperate to find and retain good staff, from managers and servers to cooks and bussers. The easy hiring days just after the Great Recession, when people were desperate for jobs, are long over. A decade ago, recalls Rick Strutz, he could post a job opening at the Deli and receive fifty to a hundred applications, all from people who knew Zingerman's philosophy and were eager to work there. By 2021, with the pandemic causing people to shy away from public-facing jobs, he was lucky to get three applicants, a situation echoed not only by businesses across student-dependent Ann Arbor, but around the country, too, as restaurants struggled to find employees despite a surge of customer business.

Because of all the pressures facing restaurants, Weinzweig says training has never been more important. "There are a lot of jobs where people are required to get a formal education," he says. But restaurants "are an industry where you can get in without any formal training. People are trained on the fly by people who don't know what they're doing."

He and the other Zingerman's managing partners saw an opportunity to change that in 1994. In the process, ZingTrain has spread Zingerman's management philosophies far beyond Ann Arbor. Rick Bayless, one of ZingTrain's earliest customers, is convinced that the training program— not Zingerman's food—speaks loudest for the company within the industry. "To me, when you say Zingerman's out in the restaurant world, away from Ann Arbor, they would say ZingTrain," he says of his fellow restaurant owners.

THE BIRTH OF ZINGTRAIN

ZingTrain came to life a dozen years after the Deli opened, the same year that Saginaw and Weinzweig published their first vision for the company, and coincided with the launch of the Bakehouse. The first managing partner was Maggie Bayless (no relation to Rick), who had worked with Saginaw, Weinzweig, and Frank Carollo at Maude's, and who also was an early staffer at the Deli.

With input from the founders and participation from many of the managing partners, Maggie Bayless built an impressive training operation. It offered classes at its offices in Zingerman's South, custom training sessions conducted either in Ann Arbor or at a client's business, and beginning in 2020, virtual sessions. About half the companies that use Zing-Train were restaurants and food companies, but the other half ranged from banks and hospitals to marketing firms.

Whether in person or online, the sessions usually kick off with a short lecture by a member of Zingerman's staff, or an expert brought in to discuss a particular topic. The principles that are the focus of the class are outlined. There can be exercises on paper and brainstorming with seat-mates and the people seated nearby. And, there's an opportunity for the people taking part to come up with ideas that they can apply to their own companies, or to the way they manage and work. In-person classes featured lots of Zingerman's coffee and pastries from the Bakehouse across the street to fuel the conversations.

While it might seem that the fallout from #MeToo would have generated significant business for ZingTrain, Weinzweig says it didn't. For one thing, abusive managers may not want to go through the self-examination that happens at ZingTrain. "Most of the people who need [training] and decide to get it are going for stock training," he says. "Those are good things, but too much is being done to get somebody off their back than because they believe in the work."

Others may not want to pay what ZingTrain charges. Individual in-person courses can cost $1,250, although there is a discount for booking multiple seats in a class. Boston-based chef Joanne Chang says she spent $13,000 to send her group of eight managers to Ann Arbor in 2019, including $8,000 for classes, and the rest for airfare, hotels, and meals. At that point, digital learning was not a focus; since the pandemic, it has become ZingTrain's primary way of reaching customers.

Like the restaurant owners and chefs who borrow ideas from each other, ZingTrain also looks elsewhere for inspiration. Just before the pandemic, it introduced a class called How to Improve, which is based on the concepts of continuous improvement and eliminating waste that are part of the Toyota Way, the car company's heralded production method. It is taught by Tom Root, the former Toyota executive who helped bring some order into Mail Order.

However, the core lineup is made up of courses that exemplify the Zingerman's approach. The curriculum is composed of five main types of classes: customer service, leadership development, Visioning, Open Book Management, and Bottom Line Training. Every participant receives "recipes" like those used at Zingerman's—tangible, easy to implement tools that are aimed at improving a company's bottom line. The classes are also an opportunity for the students to network (a little easier to do in person than on-screen) and build their contacts.

In-person courses include visits to Zingerman's businesses. Along with instruction and class materials, students in the ZingTrain classes also gain access to ZingTrain staff, who encourage them to call or email with any issues that need to be addressed.

HOW CHEFS HAVE USED ZINGTRAIN

Rick Bayless credits ZingTrain with helping his restaurants grow to $20 million a year in revenue before the pandemic, with about three hundred employees. Back in 1997, Bayless got in touch with Weinzweig to help with employee training. He and his wife, Deeann, his business partner, had trained staff themselves, but as they expanded, he realized they were too busy to continue teaching on their own. Besides, training was not their first love, and it clearly was something where the Zingerman's crew shone. "Ari had an approach to business that was similar to ours, but he boxed it up in a way that people could see it less amorphously," Bayless says.

At that time, many corporate training programs didn't take into account the special circumstances that restaurants faced, he says, from the constant pressures of customer service to the complexities of managing staffs from many different backgrounds. "When you hear people talk about business, it's from the big corporate perspective," Bayless says. "Ari is really good at bringing values in. A lot of people in the food business are really passionate about the project that they have. They're like artists. The idea of getting into the restaurant business to get rich doesn't really [define] the people I know."

The initial ZingTrain session that Bayless attended was on Visioning. He admits that this is not his strong suit. "I couldn't write a five- or ten- or fifteen-year vision for love or money," he jokes. But he is an advocate for Zingerman's philosophy of Open Book Management, in which financial information that normally would be kept confidential is shared with employees. While he can't quantify the effects of ZingTrain in dollar terms, Bayless says it has paid off enormously in helping him retain staff, some of whom had been with his restaurants for twenty-five to thirty years.

"We're all on the same team. It's better if everybody knows what's going on," Bayless says. "The thing we've always done is track our costs.

I'm not great at all of that, but I know, having been raised in a family-run restaurant, you have to watch all of that." He continues, "You would never call me a passionate businessman, but if you don't mind the business part of it, you can't do that stuff that you want to do. I'm not motivated by doing things cheaper, I'm motivated by being able to do it." Before employees are hired, Bayless and his managers talk to them about their motivations. As soon as they come on board, "they learn the nuts and bolts of the operation. Without the nuts and bolts, they will fall flat on their faces," he says.

Essentially, he runs his restaurants according to Zingerman's Guiding Principles, although Bayless has adapted them to work in his Chicago restaurants. "I rewrote them and rewrote them and rewrote them and put them in language our staff could understand," Bayless says. "There's a certain Ann Arbor thing that permeates all the Zingerman's stuff. I don't think it lives very well outside Ann Arbor."

FINDING A PURPOSE

But adapting its teachings is exactly what ZingTrain expects its clients to do—and it has happened over and over again across the restaurant world. ZingTrain has helped Alon Shaya, the award-winning restaurant owner in New Orleans and Denver, get a fresh start. Shortly after winning a James Beard Award in 2017 for his namesake restaurant, Shaya, he was fired by the Besh Organization, after he privately and publicly voiced his concerns about the harassment of female employees by company managers and allegedly Besh himself. Despite a rising profile in the national restaurant world, Shaya couldn't start a business under his own name. A judge ruled that the Besh group legally owned the rights to it. So, the separation meant he had to begin from scratch.

Shaya decided to launch two new restaurants in 2018: Saba in New

Orleans, and Safta in Denver (the names mean "grandfather" and "grandmother" in Hebrew). Before the first meals were served, ZingTrain conducted sessions for his managers. Most importantly, the Zingerman's trainers stressed ways for Shaya's staff to conduct business with respect for customers and each other. The restaurants use Open Book Management and hold weekly huddles at which the Zingerman's principles are reinforced. The principles for his organization are painted on walls that servers and kitchen staff pass every day. His staff members also frequently attend off-site events that are meant to instill collegiality.

"We share all our numbers, revenues, profits, losses, operating procedures," Shaya says. "No matter what position you're in, you can make a contribution and be rewarded for it and be part of the decision making."

Shaya's enthusiasm for Zingerman's principles stems from a car ride he took with Weinzweig in 2017. They were on their way to a symposium on Jewish food held at the University of North Carolina, sponsored by the Carolina Center for Jewish Studies. But Shaya knew about Zingerman's years before that. "I am a huge Deli fan, and I would follow everything they do," he says. He had Zingerman's management books on his shelf and routinely connected with Weinzweig at Southern Foodways conferences. "I was very fascinated by him and the company he built and their approach," he says.

To the outside world, it seemed Shaya was a success and the envy of other New Orleans chefs. But inside, he was miserable. "I was going through a point in my career where I was trying to identify how to move forward based on values versus based on what my idea of success was prior to that," he says. During the talk with Weinzweig, "I was explaining to him how I was at a crossroad. Even though I was part of a successful restaurant, I wasn't happy. I didn't feel like I belonged. I felt like I needed more substance in my life. He helped me get my thoughts in line."

Shaya learned, "You have to define what happiness is for you, and work toward that. It's really when so much for me started to change. I started putting my focus on the things I believed in and the things that made me happy as a human and a husband. It was like waiting for an award to come through, or a full book of reservations. Those things were important to me, and it wasn't necessarily making me happy." Within a short time, "I was able to make great changes. I have a sense of equilibrium when I talk to [Weinzweig]. He has a really special outlook in how he views success and how he views business. I felt like I [hadn't been] surrounding myself with people I really admired and respected."

One of the lessons he learned from Weinzweig was a story about plastic bags. "He started talking about a plastic bag that is being pushed through the air, and being affected by all its surroundings, and having no control over what direction it's going to go." What Weinzweig meant was that in business, distractions can come along at any moment, and without a clear focus, a business can be pushed in ways out of its control. "I thought, I don't want to be that plastic bag. I don't want to be told what to think and where to go and what to pay attention to," he says. "I came back saying, 'We need to control our bag. We need to take control and make sure it lands where it wants to land.'"

Shaya is determined to change the experience that many people encounter in the restaurant business, where a military-style kitchen hierarchy has long been present. "I was managed through fear and intimidation through so much of my career," he says. "As a young chef, you tend to start thinking that's the way it has to be. You become empowered in a way that's destructive. You might be able to cook well, but the real reason you're in that position is because you want to control and influence in a way that is beneficial to you. It's so much of what causes that toxicity."

But by embracing Zingerman's principles for his own restaurant group, Pomegranate, "Everything we've done has to help curb those stereotypes and help think of ways we can manage that is empowering for good and that is respectful and educational," he says. "Our core values are respect, and empowering and fairness. The people who are put in positions of influence are the people we can all look to for respect and guidance that lines up with our core values. If you're going to become the chef at Saba, it's because you're a talented, driven, kind, rational person. Not because you make the best omelet."

Shaya has a huge opportunity to test his application of Zingerman's principles with a splashy new restaurant in New Orleans. In 2021, he opened Miss River, the lead restaurant in the new Four Seasons Hotel and Private Residences on New Orleans's riverfront. It's part of a $530 million renovation of the landmark World Trade Center, which has been closed for two decades. Shaya's newest place offers his take on classic New Orleans dishes, with an emphasis on Gulf seafood, vegetables, and other locally sourced fare. As a condition of the project, which was under discussion for several years, Shaya insisted that he be able to incorporate the principles that he crafted from his relationship with Zingerman's. "I look at them as mentors and teachers that will always be there for us."

BOTTOM LINE CHANGE IN ACTION

If Alon Shaya has found fame in part through his application of Zingerman's principles, millennial Memphis bakery owner Kat Gordon credits them for giving her a start in the food business. She admits she knew absolutely nothing about running a business when she opened Muddy's Bake Shop in Memphis on Leap Day, 2008. "It's not something you would recommend to anyone you care about," Gordon says, laughing. "Oh, sure, open a small business in a recession and do it in a field where you have no background, and do it with no money." She liked to bake cookies and cakes in her spare time, and found it far more interesting than her day jobs selling real estate and working retail.

So, despite a warning from her parents, and with her friends' encouragement, she decided to take the plunge. Naming the bakery after her grandmother, she managed a build out for around $30,000, taking over what had been a coffee shop that lacked a commercial kitchen. Rather than do an immediate renovation, she installed what was basically a souped-up residential kitchen. "I'd never used a stand mixer. I bought a KitchenAid after I signed the lease," she says. "I really thought the lesson God had for me in this was for me to fail." Within weeks, there were lines out the door for her wares, including her specialty, the Prozac Cupcake (devil's food cake with a light butter cream icing), chocolate chip cookies, and Plain Jane cake, a vanilla layer cake with vanilla butter cream.

After amassing a pile of admiring press clippings and sterling online reviews, Muddy's eventually expanded into three locations (customers could shop at two, while the other was a prep kitchen), and took on fifty-nine staff members. She wound up 2019 with revenues of $2.5 million. And ZingTrain played a key role in her success.

Gordon already knew the Zingerman's story when she first encountered Weinzweig at a food conference. But rather than her approaching him, he came to the Muddy's table and asked if he could sit with the young bakers. "Our table was the one that looked like it didn't belong there," she says. "Everyone else was dressed for a business meeting. You could see me across the room with my pink hair." Gordon had browsed the ZingTrain class list but had not signed up because she had no spare profits to pay for training. After meeting Weinzweig, however, she decided to start with the course on Bottom Line Change.

Says Gordon, "Everybody starts with Visioning, and Zingerman's gets a lot of street cred because of Visioning, but if I were designing the order [of classes], Bottom Line Change is the one I would have them take first. You can come home and make even a tiny improvement. If you don't have the maturity yet to know who you are and what you do well, suddenly jumping into the deep end of that pool with the best of intentions, you could attempt to imitate and not adapt. Bottom Line Change is such a boots-on-the-ground class."

Gordon admits that she was skeptical about Visioning when she first encountered the idea. "Like a lot of people, my first reaction was 'Hmm,'" she says. "Then my English-major self said, 'Ooooo, literature. Storytelling.'" In 2015, she wrote a vision for her bakeries for 2020. In retrospect, she thinks she relied too much on staff input and not enough on her own instincts. "Visioning for individuals versus Visioning in groups is really different. Knowing the organization is necessary to use the tool well," she says. "The first group vision we wrote was feeling I had learned just enough to do it, and now let's do a five-year vision."

But, Gordon says, "I don't have a partner, I don't have managing partners, it is just me. I do like to have more control. I actually have a really strong hand in our creative process. The mistake I made was thinking that we had to be more consensus driven. It sounded great, but it was a whole lot of wishes from the staff that didn't have enough temperament from me. I'm the one that's going to be here in five years. I'm the one whose mortgage is on the line. I took myself out of it too much."

Still, flawed or not, that vision led to her own teaching activities. Taking part in a book club with other Memphis small-business owners, she began to talk about the brainstorming that she had done with her staff. One of the book club members asked if Gordon would teach a Visioning seminar at her company. "Not only did Maggie [Bayless] really encourage me to offer it, but she also encouraged me to charge for it," Gordon says. In fall 2020, she began to offer a virtual Visioning course to the public, alongside the virtual baking classes she created in order to offset the impact of the pandemic. Her approach differs, depending on the people who sign up. "If I'm working with a group that wants a team vision, we draw a Venn diagram. It includes what you want; what your customers want; what your staff wants. And the written vision is where it falls in the middle," she says.

Gordon believes that she's "a better business owner, and a better manager and a better human for having had anything to do with ZingTrain."

Now in her late thirties, she says, "You grow a lot in the twenty-five to thirty-five age range. That's the decade of 'holy cow,' a lot of change, and growth and maturity. Without exaggeration, I really think ZingTrain for me was a really big part of it." Since she began taking classes at age twenty-eight, "I really just feel like ZingTrain has made an impact on my business and even on me. Even my marriage—how different would my marriage be? We took Open Book principles and put them into our marriage. We do a quarterly family meeting. We end with appreciation. I think that influence has been a really big one and a positive one."

In 2021, Gordon found herself having to rethink Muddy's once more. She wrote a fresh vision, this time only good for a year, in which she outlined goals for her much-changed baking business. "We identified the things that we felt proud of. The things we're enjoying. And the things we want to take with us into our future." From her three outlets, she condensed to her Memphis original headquarters. But she launched a construction project that included a larger kitchen as well as a dedicated space for teaching classes and holding events. The revised approach let her focus on the two areas that meant most to her: sharing sweets as well as ideas. She told her customers, "It's been a labor of love and we are so freakin' proud of it, excited for it, and above all, ready to *get to work MAKING IT reality* for YOU to enjoy!"

In all corners of the United States, other restaurant staff members also have learned Zingerman's principles. Eight managers from Flour Bakery and Café, the Boston group run by James Beard Award–winning pastry chef Joanne Chang, took classes at ZingTrain in early 2019. They were the third group of employees that Chang had sent to Ann Arbor, including front-of-the-house managers and pastry chefs. In addition, Weinzweig has come to Boston twice to train groups of Flour staff.

The 2019 group learned "how to effect change, and help their teams to be more profitable," Chang says. "We are growing pretty quickly at this point, and we need all the help we can get to be more efficient and more effective." Not long after the staffers returned to Boston, Chang opened her eighth Flour Bakery, and she is now up to ten businesses. Although she's also received many opportunities to expand in other cities, she expects to keep her operations rooted in Boston, just as Zingerman's has maintained its base in Ann Arbor.

For Rick Bayless, the biggest benefit from ZingTrain has been that "it helps me sleep at night," he says. "ZingTrain has equipped us with a common understanding and language that I can share. And if something falls apart," he says, "it means I don't have to feel I'm the only one here trying to keep everything upright."

Back at my dinner in New Orleans, I couldn't help an occasional glance at Ella Brennan and her party, who were chatting with the servers and looking over their food with experienced eyes. I saw her lift a fork to her mouth, consider what she was eating, and nod approvingly. It was just the kind of feedback that would give a sense of satisfaction to any chef. Her daughter says Weinzweig's perpetual focus on learning reminds her of her mother. "Just face it, you've got to work hard," Martin says. "But you've got to get joy from that."

CHAPTER TWELVE

Camp Bacon and Guests

No Zingerman's event name evokes a smile more than Camp Bacon (assuming you're a carnivore, that is). "You mean they really have a camp—with bacon?" people have asked me. Well, no, people aren't sleeping in tents hugging rashers of meat to their chests. But since 2009, Camp Bacon has been Zingerman's signature special event.

Billed as "bacon for the brain, belly and soul," Camp Bacon has grown from a modest fund-raiser to include five days of baking classes, a luncheon, a film festival, a street fair, a special dinner called the Bacon Ball, and the Main Event, a day of seminars on food topics. Whichever event you attend, bacon is the centerpiece, and if you go to the seminars held on the day of the Main Event, you'll be served bacon or pork products for breakfast and lunch, and as samples for snacks throughout the day.

What bred Zingerman's devotion to bacon? Its attention coincided with America's culinary obsession with the product. By the mid-2000s, Weinzweig had become one of the country's leading proponents of bacon, such as the varieties made by the Nueske family and the small-batch bacons produced by Allan Benton at Benton's Country Hams in Madisonville, Tennessee.

In 2009, Weinzweig published the *Zingerman's Guide to Better Bacon*, in which he dubbed bacon "the olive oil of America." The book traced bacon's roots to medieval England, where it was used to promote marital harmony. "I wanted to help consumers understand the difference between good and bad bacon, to hear the amazing stories of the country's great artisan bacon curers, and to learn how to effectively employ bacon varieties in different culinary applications," Weinzweig wrote in a Zingerman's newsletter.

In the front of the bacon book, he mentioned his idea of holding an imaginary Camp Bacon, where all the indoor and outdoor activities would center on bacon. It was an exotic idea for a boy who attended a kosher camp as a kid. A couple of months after the book was published, Pete Sickman-Garner, who then handled Zingerman's marketing, joked that the company ought to make Camp Bacon a reality, envisioning it as a fund-raiser to help local and national charities.

And with that, Camp Bacon was born. The concept, according to Weinzweig, was to eat a lot of good bacon and to learn how to prepare it properly. Zingerman's teaches four different methods, using the oven, a cast-iron skillet, a campfire, and yes, a microwave, which is my favorite option. At the sessions, carnivores could meet like-minded people who were interested in bacon, and food in general. Zingerman's also raised money for the charitable organizations involved in the camp, built a community, and most of all gave participants a fun time.

Camp Bacon has become intertwined with Southern Foodways Alliance, a nonprofit group studying Southern culture that is based at the Center for the Study of Southern Culture at the University of Mississippi in Oxford. In 1998, then–graduate student John T. Edge organized the first Southern Foodways symposium, and the organization kicked off a year later. Since then, SFA's annual symposium has attracted food producers, purveyors, writers, and food lovers from across the United States and around the world. Its growth coincided with the rise of the artisanal food movement, and its films, podcasts, oral histories, and other publications have been instrumental in preserving the history of American food. In 2020, however, Southern Foodways became the subject of intense criticism from members of the Black food community, who felt that the organization had capitalized on African American stories but was not sufficiently diverse. The university pledged to conduct an outside review of the organization's staff and activities, and Edge stepped aside as day-to-day director.

Edge remembers meeting Weinzweig at an SFA program and was fascinated to see his interest in the topics being discussed. "For the first few years, I got to know Ari as the guy sitting close to the front with a yellow legal pad taking furious notes, learning and interpreting things he could take back to Ann Arbor," Edge recalls. "Watching Ari watch a room, and watching Ari listen, you hear gears moving and gates opening."

Weinzweig told Edge that SFA was "the food world nonprofit that most closely complemented the work of Zingerman's. That's a great compliment to us," Edge says. "The idea that we were doing something in small-town Mississippi that resonated in big-college-town Michigan meant something." Edge says SFA put on a Camp Bacon–like event of its own in Louisville in 2010, "but what Ari did was far bolder and cooler."

For me, as a food journalist, the value of Camp Bacon has always been the day of seminars and demonstrations that focus on both history and trends in the food world. Every year, I find out something new, particularly from the presentations by Susan Schwallie, executive director of the NPD Group. Her organization regularly surveys thirty thousand consumers on their dining habits, and forecasts areas where food purveyors should pay attention.

In 2019, for example, Schwallie talked about the fast-emerging field of plant-based meat, which was especially resonating among millennials and with young consumers who make up Generation Z. At the time of her talk, companies such as Beyond Meat and Impossible Foods were just beginning to become household names. Now the pair regularly introduce new lab-developed meat substitutes and are conquering the restaurant scene, from fast food to fine dining.

However, Camp Bacon's focus remains on naturally sourced food itself. Its presenters have included internationally known purveyors such as Arturo Sánchez, a Spanish company founded in 1917 that produces some of the world's finest Iberian ham, and Rusticella, the Italian pasta maker. The demonstrations have included mixing bacon-infused cocktails, cooking pasta that was subsequently sauced with bacon, and one session in which an entire hog was broken down into the parts used for cooking (not a presentation for the faint of heart).

If you happen to miss the seminars, you can often catch up to the same presenters at the Bacon Street Fair, held on the Sunday after the Main Event at the Ann Arbor Farmer's Market. That gives the local community a sense of who took part, and allows people to sample some of the foods that were part of the program. If you miss out on the week of events, don't worry. Zingerman's offers ample opportunities throughout the year to meet chefs, authors, and experts.

SPECIAL DINNERS

Interactions with chefs and cookbook authors have always been a staple of the culinary world. Whether on television or in person, culinary presentations fascinate cooks of all ages, backgrounds, and genders. Zingerman's capitalizes on this interest in several ways, and one of the most popular is the special dinners, primarily held at the Roadhouse. Prior to the pandemic, these typically took place monthly, and by the time the shutdown was in place, it had held nearly 250 of them and Weinzweig is eager to see them resume.

These nights offer multiple benefits. For the chefs and authors who travel to Ann Arbor, Zingerman's offers an opportunity to expand their brands beyond their home territory, meet their fans, and perhaps sell a few cookbooks. For the diners, it's a chance to meet notable names in the food business, learn their methods, and taste their food the way they intend it to be prepared. For the Zingerman's staff, it allows them to see some of the best practitioners in the business up close. Everyone learns something: The chefs see how Zingerman's operates. The diners and students are educated, and the staff gets a basis for comparison between the Zingerman's philosophy and how another chef or writer might operate.

"It can be very powerful," says cookbook author and culinary educator Molly Stevens, who took part in the first special dinner at Zingerman's Roadhouse and has returned several times since. Stevens and Weinzweig have been friends almost as long as the Deli has been around. She originally encountered Weinzweig in 1986, when she was teaching at the French Culinary Institute in New York City. In an era before the internet, they would exchange postcards and letters, and connect when Weinzweig made buying trips to the East Coast. "We were both starting out, and finding our way," Stevens recalls. "Obviously, we've done different things," but the pair shared a philosophy and an interest in food.

With their mutual friend, the late cheese expert Daphne Zepos, they took trips, hunting down interesting products and learning about the way foods were made. Once it opened, Zingerman's Roadhouse seemed a perfect place for Stevens to teach her expertise. For that first special dinner, Alex Young, then the executive chef at the Roadhouse, suggested a menu that drew from recipes in *One Potato, Two Potato*, a cookbook that Stevens coauthored with Roy Finamore. He listened to her suggestions and paid an impressive amount of attention to detail in mapping out how the food would be prepared. "He invited his potato farmer," Stevens says, marveling. "That was really fun, really exciting." Stevens says the Zingerman's staff made her feel like more than a visitor. "It's not just some celebrity who's in our kitchen," Stevens says. "It's really fun to be part of the group. I don't think I've had that experience in other restaurants."

According to Stevens, the special dinner process goes something like this. Months in advance, she connects with Roadhouse chef Bob Bennett to fix a date for the event. Then they begin brainstorming about a theme, checking to see what kind of seasonal produce might be available. Her 2019 book, *All About Dinner,* includes recipes for appetizers, main courses, side dishes, and desserts. So, she and Bennett came up with a six-part menu. It began with an *amuse-bouche* of *lecso*, a Hungarian-style topping made from slow-cooked peppers and tomatoes, served on Zingerman's sage-and-walnut bread. The starter was *lablabi*, a Tunisian chickpea stew, followed by roasted carrots with pistachios, sumac, and a yogurt-lime drizzle (I immediately added those carrots to my cooking repertoire). The main course was a choice of spice-rubbed flank steak or a vegetarian entrée of eggplant with ricotta, spinach, and basil, and the dinner wound up with a pear, dried apricot, and ginger crisp.

Stevens says the recipes might have to be adapted a little for a crowd of a hundred people, since they were originally written for home cooks. But she is there to make sure any changes fit with her intent. On the day of her 2019 dinner, Stevens arrived, met the staff, went over the menu, and then took part in the Roadhouse's weekly huddle. She's fascinated with the way Zingerman's operates. "One of the things that's so amazing is the whole Open Book [Management] thing," Stevens says. "That's not just performance. It's real. It's incredible to watch it in action."

When the meeting ended, Stevens got out of the staff's way while they prepared her dishes. (Not every visitor does this. At one Zingerman's dinner, scheduled to end at 9 p.m., the service stretched on for another ninety minutes because the guest chef insisted on plating every dish.) "I'm very clear: This is your team, I'm honored, and I will be there, and help a little bit, and I'm definitely on call for whatever," she says. However, "I learned that as much fun as it is to do these things, my job is to be an author."

Chicago author and poet Audrey Petty began her own association with Zingerman's in 2003, when she took part in an SFA panel on race and food. She read a now-celebrated essay ("Late Night Chitlins with Momma") on chitlins, or pork intestines, a traditional dish among African

American cooks whose preparation can be fragrant and time-consuming. "Ours came frozen solid in a red plastic bucket," wrote Petty, whose essay was later published by *Saveur* magazine and included in a volume of the country's best food writing. "Butchered and packaged by Armour. Ten pounds in all. Cleaned, they'd reduce to much less, not even filling my mother's cast-iron pot. We usually shared them in the wintertime, Momma and I. Negotiations regarding their appearance began weeks in advance, around the dinner table. My mother would tell my father she was considering fixing chitlins for the holidays. My father would groan, twist his mouth, and protest in vain. 'Why you got to be cooking them?'"

Weinzweig liked her essay so much that he read it out loud two years later at Zingerman's first African American dinner, a celebration of Black culture and foodways, which became an annual event. Their friendship sparked Petty's own enthusiasm for Zingerman's. "I may have heard about it prior to meeting Ari, but when I met Ari, I started looking to Zingerman's as a source for gifts and food," she says. Petty vowed, "I'm going to make a pilgrimage to Zingerman's at one point in my life."

Her opportunity came in 2011, when Weinzweig invited her to be the featured speaker at the seventh annual African American dinner and to devise a menu. Petty had lost her mother earlier that year and decided that the menu would be a tribute to her. She found the experience to be both melancholy and celebratory. "It's for sure that my imagined Zingerman's met the actual reality of Zingerman's," Petty says. "It was really lovely, fun, warm, and informative. I was met with generosity and care and co-grappling with some of the things I was writing about for the first time."

BAKING CLASSES

Across Ann Arbor, the Bakehouse has also hosted a series of events with some of the country's most notable baking experts. These classes and demonstrations, called Bake!, began in August 2006. The idea was simple: Take the mystery out of baking and inspire people to do so at home. The events take place in teaching kitchens across a courtyard from the Bakehouse operations and retail store. Amy Emberling, the Bakehouse's managing partner, hoped that the students would engage with each other, and that Zingerman's would create an avid community of home bakers.

The original Bake! classes were taught by Emberling, Frank Carollo, and bakers Amy Small and Alejandro Ramon. Attendance was light at some of the first events, but the baking sessions began to grow in popularity as word of mouth about the classes spread. By 2021, Bake! had taught as many as fifty thousand students in fifteen years. During demonstrations, students watch an expert make an item, then sample the result. In the hands-on instruction, participants get to make the bread or pastry themselves. The Bake! series has a regular rotation of sixty-five topics, from savory classes that focus on cuisines like Mexican, classes on pizza and full breakfasts, and on pastries, pie, cake, flatbreads, marshmallows, and one of the most popular, holiday cookies (or Fancy Schmancy Cookies, in Zingerman's nomenclature).

In a given year, Bake! was teaching about six thousand classes, and contributed about 8 percent of the Bakehouse's revenue, says Emberling. "Although it's a small part of our business, it's very important in terms of relationship to the community," Emberling says. Essentially, if something is popular at the Bakehouse, it's likely that you can learn to bake it in a class. When the pandemic forced Zingerman's to close down in-person classes, Bake! went virtual, including a version of Fancy Schmancy Cookies that included a baking kit with premeasured ingredients. In-person classes returned in 2021.

While the classes originally were meant for adults, Zingerman's eventually created a separate series for families and for young people to take part in. There are private classes, classes that are created as wedding or shower activities, and Bake-cations, days-long or week-long classes that focus on specific types of baking. The Bake! classes engage "a different group of customers, and they often shop in our store, and other Zingerman's stores," Emberling says. Through the years, I've taken about a dozen Bake! classes, including Italian cookies, flatbreads, and a Thanksgiving pie class that reduced me to tears.

It wasn't the instructors' fault: I have always had trouble working with pie dough. I simply have been unable to master the technique of rolling out a perfect circle. My mother never made pie from scratch, and I've had trouble as an adult figuring out the proper technique. I was assured that I was far from the only person who cried over their pie, and I was patiently coached in how to roll, lift, and drape my pie dough over my pan. While my pies weren't exactly ready for Instagram close-ups, they still got devoured at Thanksgiving dinner. I learned the difference between an all-butter crust, one with lard, and one that combined the two. Even if patched together, the pies tasted just fine.

Some of the most popular Bake! classes have featured baking superstars, such as Stella Parks, a baking expert at Serious Eats who is known for her cookbook *BraveTart: Iconic American Desserts*, and culinary legend Dorie Greenspan, the closest person my generation has to a Julia Child of baking. Greenspan and I met years ago via email, before social media made it easy for people to connect and stay in touch. I admired Greenspan's articles for the *New York Times* and the *Washington Post,* and she was a fan of my writing for the *Times*. We subsequently met when I worked for NPR in Boston, and I was delighted in 2016 when Greenspan conducted a Bake! demonstration, teaching the audience how to make her famous jammers, a jam-filled cookie baked in a muffin tin, and her delectable chocolate World Peace cookies.

Sitting next to me for Dorie's class was Ina Pinkney, who had owned Ina's, a café in Chicago that specialized in breakfast. Although Ina's closed in 2013, the café lives on in the documentary *Breakfast at Ina's*, as well as in Pinkney's cookbook *Ina's Kitchen*. Pinkney knew Weinzweig from a presentation he made to the Chicago chapter of Les Dames d'Escoffier, the organization for women in the culinary world, of which I am a member. Pinkney has conducted dozens of her own demonstrations over the years, keeping two drawers in her kitchen with the equipment she needs to appear in front of an audience.

Watching Greenspan's class, "I was so moved by the sensibility of it, and the gentleness of it," Pinkney says. She was impressed by "the organization of how classes were held. The way people in the audience responded. They were getting their money's worth and getting so much more." During breaks from Greenspan's teaching, Pinkney received ample attention from her own fans, who remembered her from her Chicago restaurant. Emberling subsequently invited her to teach her own Bake! class and asked if she would be willing to come for two days.

Compared with the bare-bones treatment she had sometimes received elsewhere, Pinkney says the Zingerman's crew was "so professional, without any stiffness or pretense." When she arrived, "I went right into the kitchen. They showed me a sheet pan with the ingredients measured" for her Heavenly Hots pancakes, a signature feature at her restaurant. The recipe was written on the parchment paper that sat beneath the ingredients. Says Pinkney, "I always bring the recipe. But to have it written out was heaven."

Pinkney and the Zingerman's staff divided up the workload so that while Pinkney was demonstrating the pancakes, the staffers were making them to distribute to the audience. Says Pinkney, "I remember feeling cared for and respected. I'm not Dorie Greenspan. I wasn't on my home turf. But I was treated like Dorie Greenspan."

ABOUT THE BRIDE AND GROOM

But people needn't be Greenspan or Pinkney to experience Zingerman's special treatment. During the past twenty years, Zingerman's has opened several dedicated events spaces available to the public for meetings, meals, and weddings, among other occasions.

One of its first efforts was in the Kerrytown Market area, at a restaurant that had changed hands many times. Once called the Kerrytown Bistro, it subsequently became Eve's, run by Eve Aronoff Fernandez, a Zingerman's alumni and *Top Chef* contestant. When she opened another restaurant in downtown Ann Arbor, Zingerman's took over the lease and turned it first into an events space, and then into Miss Kim, a Korean restaurant opened by Ji Hye Kim. She had read about Zingerman's when I wrote about it in the *New York Times* in 2007 and sought a job at the Roadhouse. That turned into a food truck, San Street, financed in part by Zingerman's (Dancing Sandwich Enterprises still retains the trademark) and subsequently her restaurant, largely owned by Zingerman's, but operated under her name. A few blocks away, Zingerman's helped transform Ann Arbor's empty bus station downtown into Greyline, a cavernous rental space with a long bar and the ability to host groups of up to a hundred and fifty people seated at tables, or two hundred for a cocktail party.

But the jewel of Zingerman's events spaces is Cornman Farms, the historic property in Dexter, Michigan, where Tabitha Mason became a managing partner. Before the pandemic, Cornman was building a reputation as one of the area's most elegant spots for weddings. And while the pandemic initially halted and then severely limited the size of such gatherings, people who were able to hold them said the experience was unforgettable.

Stephanie Ostling Mason, a North Carolina pharmacist, toured Cornman with her mother in 2019, even before her husband, Matt, formally proposed. Knowing that her engagement was imminent, Ostling Mason wanted to choose a venue early, because desirable places were booking up eighteen months to two years in advance. She and her now-husband were from Michigan and wanted to get married in the state. Both were Zingerman's fans from their time at the University of Michigan, although their limited student budgets meant they couldn't indulge that often. "When we hear Zingerman's, we know what Zingerman's means—quality food, quality service, and we know they are going to deliver what they promise to do," Ostling Mason says.

She and her mother received a full tour of the property and discussed options with Tabitha Mason and other staff members. Although she had planned to look at other places, Cornman wound up being the only property that Ostling Mason considered. "They were willing to work with us in whatever they needed us to do [in order] to bring our big day to life. We felt they were in it with us," she says. Ostling Mason said the Cornman staff helped alleviate the stress through multiple phone calls, emails, and texts.

The experience made her even more appreciative of Zingerman's service philosophy. "We felt not just like customers, but like part of the family of Zingerman's," Ostling Mason says. "They made it truly about the bride and groom."

And the relationship has continued since their wedding ceremony. While Matt Mason wasn't a coffee drinker when they met, he's now a "coffee snob" who will call Zingerman's Coffee to ask questions of the baristas. Stephanie has become an avid user of Mail Order, sending her maid of honor an Italian dinner kit as her thank-you gift, and dispatching coffee, cheese, and other products to her friends. "When I was a pharmacy student, I didn't have the income to go to Zingerman's very often," she says. "Now I can enjoy it a lot more."

Zingerman's role in some of Ann Arbor's premier events came to a halt when the pandemic hit, although by 2021, it was beginning to welcome brides, chefs, and students back to Ann Arbor. Before that, it had to address the biggest crisis of its nearly four decades in business.

PART FIVE

Looking Ahead

Zingerman's Next Door sells coffee and pastries and provides seating for
customers at the Deli next door. (Courtesy of Zingerman's)

CHAPTER THIRTEEN

The Pandemic Strikes

When I began writing this book in early 2020, I planned to focus on Zingerman's history, its management principles, and the future that it saw for itself. But the arrival of the coronavirus in the United States, and its deadly spread in Michigan, forced Zingerman's to reinvent itself in a way it hadn't done since the 1990s, when its first vision was written, and gave me a different aspect of the story to tell.

Like numerous other food businesses, Zingerman's had to dismiss staff, adopt new sanitary protocols, limit hours, and make repeated menu changes in order to maintain operations. COVID itself struck Zingerman's, too, when Saginaw and Mangigian both contracted it in Las Vegas, where Saginaw was opening his new deli, Saginaw's, with help from a troop of Zingerman's friends.

While the bruising it took from the pandemic won't easily be forgotten, the company has regrouped and has recovered its lost revenue. Though every corner of Zingerman's had to be overhauled, some were deluged with more business than they could have ever imagined.

As I explained in Chapter 1, Michigan imposed its first stay-at-home order in March 2020, and the impact was swift. Overnight, ZCoB shrank from a $70 million enterprise, on a steady path to achieving $75 million in sales, to one doing about $45 million in annual revenue, Weinzweig says. That represented an immediate 35 percent decline in revenue.

Some pieces of Zingerman's were hit even harder. ZingTrain's income vanished almost completely, as did business at Catering, which typically boomed in spring and summer due to commencement parties and weddings. Cornman Farms had to cancel months of events, as did Greyline. Food Tours scrapped its 2020 schedule of trips. Indoor service halted at the Roadhouse, Miss Kim, the Deli and the businesses at Zingerman's South. All those expensive building renovations across the company seemed to have been for naught: No one could come through the doors to see them.

Says Saginaw, "What certainly stands out to me is how some [of our] businesses were helped by it, and some were absolutely crushed." The situation painted a picture of something he and Weinzweig had spent thirty-eight years, up until 2020, trying to avoid: a group of haves and have-nots. At the very least, they hoped all the businesses could be modestly profitable, no matter their size. But the pandemic sepearated the ZCoB businesses into three categories: strong players, those that were holding their own, and the rest in peril. "If we were more financially integrated between the businesses, that wealth could have been spread around. But we're not," Saginaw says.

Not knowing what might happen as the pandemic spread, Saginaw prepared for the worst. As soon as the statewide shutdown took effect, he made a series of phone calls to friends and potential investors to line up millions of dollars in loans in case Zingerman's needed them, essentially creating a line of credit. He even got in touch with a contact in the private equity world to explore whether there would be interest in buying Zingerman's intellectual property, if the situation grew so dire that the company's very existence was threatened.

"That would have been our last, dying gasp," Saginaw says. "We would only do it because it would be preferable to going out of business.

That's how close it was. We were looking at selling our souls rather than risk the lives of our people." Saginaw received enthusiastic assurances from potential backers that money would be there if he needed it, along with offers of lines of credit. But thankfully, for Zingerman's, things never got that bad. By the end of its fiscal year, on July 31, 2020, it had clawed its way back to annualized revenue of about $63 million. That was still a $2 million decline from the prior fiscal year, but Zingerman's avoided the sheer disaster that so many other restaurants and food businesses experienced, thanks to a Herculean effort that changed the way the founders, and many of the partners, looked at the company. For the 2021 fiscal year, Zingerman's returned to $65 million, buoyed by Mail Order, and CFO Ron Maurer says $70 million is once again within reach. Zingerman's, like numerous other food businesses, received help from the federal government under the Paycheck Protection Program. By 2021, it had received $9.8 million, which it used to pay staff salaries.

But that money alone did not preserve ZCoB. Rather than be crushed by the pandemic, Zingerman's saw it as an opportunity for reinvention.

BEING HONEST

From the beginning of the pandemic, Zingerman's was transparent with its customers, who were undoubtedly wondering what lay in store. On Thursday, March 12, 2020, I received the first email from a Zingerman's business that mentioned COVID-19 in its subject line. The message, from the Roadhouse, detailed the kind of sanitary steps the restaurant was taking to reassure already nervous customers. The following Sunday marked Zingerman's thirty-eighth anniversary, normally a time to celebrate. But inside the company, it meant something else completely.

Says the Deli's Mo Frechette, "That was the weekend when everybody looked at each other and said, 'Now it's for real.'" Although the 2008 recession had been tough on the company, no one had any experience in widespread job cuts. "You have to remember that we were always hiring," Amy Emberling says. Saginaw, looking at Zingerman's books, could see that each business was in dramatically different shape. "If I could go back, knowing what was coming, I would have an enormous amount of cash on hand," he says—enough to fund up to eighteen months of operations, if necessary.

Later that first week, the partners met for their usual huddle, now under social distancing rules. This one was much different from the casual celebratory sessions before COVID, recalls Emberling. "The one big decision that we all made together in that discussion was, 'Are we staying open? Is everybody staying open? Are some of us closing?'" she says. "Everybody was in different economic states. Everyone had different amounts of cash. All these PPP loan things"—referring to the Paycheck Protection Program—"no one knew how they were going to work."

In particular, Rick Strutz couldn't figure out how the Deli, always crowded with customers, constantly managing the Line, could function in the new environment. "I said, 'I want to close,'" he recalls, shocking the other managing partners. "The fear that staff had coming to work and serving people was real. I didn't want to be part of having someone die who worked at the Deli. Every day was hard. The Zingy-ness was gone." His fellow Deli partners agreed, and the group collectively told Weinzweig and Saginaw. But the two Zingerman's cofounders, and many of the other managing partners, fervently disagreed and pushed back—an unusual move for cofounders who typically let their managing partners lead without much interference.

For one thing, the symbolism of the Deli closing might have shaken Ann Arbor and the food community at large. For another, if the Deli were to close, it would have a ripple effect. The Deli was a significant customer for the Bakehouse, the Creamery, for Coffee, and sold many of the same products carried by Mail Order. The vertical integration of Zingerman's could be blown apart. Finally, after lengthy conversations, and weighing the pros and cons, the three Deli partners changed their minds.

"We decided we wouldn't close. I'm very glad that we didn't close," Strutz says. Adds Emberling, "We all committed early on that we would stay up. Then we agreed to certain, very broad guidelines about how to operate. And then everything else is just sort of an individual business." Saginaw says he and Weinzweig reminded the group of Zingerman's founding principles. "We tried to get everybody to remember that even though things are crazy, to think, How can we be generous? How can we still have an abundance mind-set?" From there, the ideas began to flow.

THE BAKEHOUSE

In a sense, Emberling and Carollo became ZCoB's first responders. In early March 2020, they noticed that wholesale orders from restaurants and corporate customers were dropping, even before the shutdown officially began. That business quickly vanished altogether once the stay-at-home order was issued. "About half of our wholesale customers closed within two weeks of shutdown," she says. The Bakehouse experienced an immediate 30 to 40 percent drop in business.

But silver linings soon began to appear. Even though the Bakehouse lost half its wholesale volume, those customers did not equal half its wholesale *revenue*. The absence of that business meant the company could stop producing items for which it had limited demand, such as large loaves of sandwich bread used by corporate cafeterias, as well as sandwich rolls. Carollo says streamlining the product offerings actually removed some of the stress he had been feeling.

Prior to the pandemic, the Bakehouse's business had grown so much that bakery items were still being produced after he went home for the day and before he got up in the morning. "When we shrank it back down, despite being in a pandemic, I could go to bed not worrying about some-body calling at two in the morning, saying, 'This happened,'" he recalls.

As leaders, he and Emberling were determined to serve the staff by being decisive. "There was not a lot of hesitating, and there was a fair amount of self-compassion, because the information kept changing, but we would make decisions," Emberling says. "We would say to one an-other, we are going to make the best decisions with the information we have today. And if tomorrow we find out something different, we're not going to spend any time feeling bad about our decision. We'll make an-other decision. We're just going to keep moving forward." Adds Carollo, "There was real fear and anxiety and uncertainty, both personal and for our business. I had a strong belief, we both did, that what we were doing was going to be important to the community. Businesses were deciding, 'It's too complicated, it's too hard, I'm just going to close' rather than fig-ure it out. And we felt strongly the opposite—that we had to do what we could do in a safe way."

Their attitude was justified as orders picked up. About three weeks into shutdown, demand for bread and pastries at Mail Order began to soar, as it did among local customers, and when the 2020 fiscal year ended, the Bakehouse wound up only 10 percent behind its 2019 results. Mau-rer says that the usual summer drop-off in business that the Bakehouse normally experienced did not happen in 2020 or 2021, underscoring its strength within Zingerman's and with its customers. Of the 140 employ-ees then at the Bakehouse, just 16 were let go or decided not to return out of health considerations. But the Bakehouse couldn't simply operate as it had before the pandemic.

The partners needed to designate oven space to the products that sold in the highest volume. One early decision was to temporarily eliminate bagel production, as well as pretzels. Zingerman's had proudly promoted its bagels as chewy, authentic New York City bagels. It promoted Bagel Tuesday, when customers could get six free bagels if they purchased six.

For a time, shoppers got a dozen free bagels on their birthdays. The partners had even installed a dedicated oven solely for bagels. But in summer 2020, the parts for the oven lay against a far wall on the Bakehouse floor, waiting to be taken away. Emberling and Carollo concluded that the Bakehouse couldn't give baking space over to products that only sold for $1.25 each and that went stale quickly.

Even as the Bakehouse was taking the required COVID-related sanitary steps to stay open, Emberling still wanted the retail store to be a welcoming place. Her goal was to make the protections, like Plexiglas shields and hand sanitizer, obvious enough so that customers would feel safe, "but we wanted it to then sort of disappear so that you have really good service." A trip to the bakery should feel like "a blast from the past, or a refuge from what we're experiencing." By 2021, the Bakeshop had adopted an order process that was then adopted by other parts of ZCoB.

Since the Bakeshop was considered an essential business, customers could still shop in person even when restrictions on restaurants were in place. Many waited in a socially distanced line that ran down the front of the building. They also could use an app and order their baked goods for a designated time. If they didn't want to get out of their cars, they could pull into parking spaces, let the Bakehouse know they were there, and a runner would come out with their prepaid purchases. By 2022, there was a full lineup to choose from. Bagels returned several days a week, and then were available daily, although in fewer flavors than the Bakehouse once offered, and so did Carolla's favorite menu item, pretzels.

MAIL ORDER

If other managing partners were in shock from lost business, Mail Order's partners were rattled by their immediate spike in sales, which were caught up in the sweeping trend toward online grocery. "Our demand surged to levels we had never seen in the off-season," Frechette says. "We were taking between 100 percent and 200 percent more orders" during the pandemic's first months. Mail Order ended its 2020 fiscal year with revenue of $21 million, up about 27 percent from 2019. And, for the year ending in July 2021, Mail Order had revenue of $27 million— $11 million more than it generated two years before. In that time, "we grew what we would have expected over eight to ten years," he says.

Mangigian, at Coffee and Candy, says he's in awe of what Mail Order was able to accomplish. "They're just kicking ass," he says. "It's hard to say whether they're reaping the benefits of ten years [of sales] or if people fundamentally shifted the way they were buying and shopping." But nevertheless, the business prospered.

Interestingly, the mix of products that Mail Order sold didn't really change, says Frechette, although there were a few temporary shifts. For a time, Zingerman's, like other food sellers, saw a surge in demand for flour, until "everybody discovered baking is pretty hard, and stopped," Frechette says. Meanwhile, "the gluten-free trend found its doom" as customers flocked to order wheat-based bread, pastry, and pasta. "I looked over [at the order board] to see if there was something different going on, and something we could learn from it. Basically, everything they liked, they just ordered more."

The surge meant significant delays, however. Part of the fun of ordering from Mail Order's website is clicking back to the front page, where a cartoon flying pig declares the destination of the latest order. If you get there in time, you might see yours go out. However, the Mail Order deluge meant orders could not be processed for days and sometimes even weeks. Frechette says Mail Order decided not to add more staff to speed things up, as it did at the holidays, because it couldn't tell how long the pandemic would last. "We didn't know if this was going to be a few days or a few weeks," he says.

Planning for Christmas 2020 became even more complicated, because economists were predicting a recession that could dampen sales. At the same time, many Zingerman's vendors were in trouble, especially those producing perishable products. Many lost their restaurant accounts when shutdown orders took effect, and were left with a glut of excess goods. So, Mail Order came up with ways to help. Staffers invented a Victory Cheese Box, riffing off the victory gardens that Americans planted during World Wars I and II. They also put together a random cheese box, in which buyers were sold whatever assortment was available. Mail Order's demand continued into 2021, but Frechette says he isn't sure how things will go long term, with a vaccine widely available and stores reopened.

"Will people continue to shop as much online as they did before COVID? Probably not as much. But will they do more than they did? Yes. Everyone assumes it was an accelerant" toward online shopping, he says. While Maurer believes Mail Order's boom eventually will settle down, he says the pandemic alerted a new group of customers to its lineup. "They worked hard to be efficient. They've done very well and deserved [the business] they got," says the CFO.

THE DELI

Not long after the shutdown began, managing partner Strutz walked through the empty Deli, sad that the once-lively atmosphere from shoppers and diners was gone. The Deli faced other problems, too. Its Catering business evaporated just as it would be handling countless graduation parties and weddings. For months, the white delivery trucks with the Zingerman's logo sat idle in the Community High School parking lot next door. "That was a really difficult time for me," he says.

The Deli had done a little local delivery, and it could arrange to deliver menu items to people who lived outside Ann Arbor (one staffer told me he had sent an order via Uber to Cleveland). But at the beginning of the pandemic, delivery was only 3.3 percent of its revenue, Strutz says, and couldn't make up for the lost Catering business. Distressed by the Deli's dwindling income, Strutz was startled in April 2020 when the Deli suddenly received a $20,000 order from Kelly Stafford, the wife of then Detroit Lions quarterback Matthew Stafford.

She told Zingerman's that she would pay for lunches for any essential workers who came by the Deli and showed their ID badges. Stafford spread the word on her social media accounts, and orders flowed in. Her stipend "was gone in two hours," Strutz says. The next day, she repeated the purchase, giving the Deli $40,000 in business in two days. "It turned the corner," he says. "Now we were doing something good in the community."

For three months, the Deli remained closed to all but carryout and delivery. Then, it reopened a few hours a day for grocery shopping. "There were so many things to think about," says Grace Singleton. "How are we going to deal with taking cash? How are we going to deal with greeting at the front door?" I was inadvertently the first customer to be allowed inside (I was there to chat with other shoppers, and to my surprise, found there was no wait to get in). The Deli established a cash-free carryout system for menu items. Customers called in or went online, then arrived in the courtyard on Detroit Street to collect their items.

Initially, customers were not allowed to stay and eat on the Deli grounds. Some were so eager for their food that they found spots on the Detroit Street curb, where they could sit and bite into their big sandwiches, the paper wrappings acting as place mats to catch anything that fell from between the slices of bread. By early fall, the restrictions loosened enough so that diners could occupy a limited number of tables inside, or take spots in tents erected in the Deli's courtyard. But a pause imposed by the governor in late 2020 banished indoor dining once more until 2021, and the vast rooms that once held so many excited guests, and where classes like Ari's Favorite Things were taught, remained empty.

Inside, the Deli was reconfigured so that grocery and baking products were stocked along the ramp where customers once lined up. Gone were the colorful sandwich signboards, a feature of the Deli since its founding, since no one would be looking at a wall to find the name of their favorite sandwich.

Faced with unpredictable Deli business, and with nothing for Catering to do, the partners started brainstorming how the Deli could pick up some additional customers. Singleton wondered if there was some way that the shop could "take Reubens on the road." She was inspired by a 2019 pop-up that Zingerman's put on in Chicago, attracting more than a thousand customers who lined up down the street. Within days, Zingerman's found bars, pubs, and other spots in Michigan and Toledo, Ohio, to host stops on its first Reuben Tour.

Customers prepaid for thirteen types of sandwiches, plus chips, soda, baked goods, and some deli items like hunks of Parmigiano-Reggiano cheese and sliced corned beef. A limited-edition Reuben Tour T-shirt, produced by Ann Arbor–based Underground Printing, sold out. The Deli repeated the Reuben Tour later in 2020, and subsequently created a Pie Tour, sending out a food truck loaded with savory potpies and sweet dessert pies. By 2021, Catering was picking up some lost business by offering family meal kits until demand for events returned that summer and fall.

The absence of the big menu boards with the fun sandwich names was an emotional loss, and customers mourned some of the discontinued sandwiches, like whitefish salad and roast beef. But Strutz wasn't nostalgic for them, or for the Line that once snaked through the Deli, out the front door, and around the corner. "If we never had a line again, that would make me super happy," he says. Sales of salads, noodles, and veggie dishes from the Deli case were about the same as they had been when Zingerman's took in-person orders, and the food items were now preportioned, meaning it was faster for staff to add them to an order.

The numbers weren't great: In fiscal 2021, the Deli's revenue dropped to $9.75 million, compared with $17 million for 2019. Early in the fiscal year, the Deli was forecast to lose $1 million, but it managed to cut its loss to around $300,000. Jokes Strutz, "Not losing $650,000 is almost like making money." One reason for the better results was that Deli customers quickly grew accustomed to placing orders in advance, either online or by phone. By 2021, about 88 percent of the Deli's customers pre-ordered, with the remainder placing orders once they arrived on site. "We're way, way more profitable at this level of volume without in-person ordering," Strutz says. He was optimistic that the Deli's revenue would climb above $10 million once more, aiming for about $13 million to $14 million in 2022 and beyond. That should return the Deli to profitability, minus the crowds that the brick building once held. Says Strutz, "It's no longer a mosh pit experience."

THE ROADHOUSE

Although sit-down dining is its stock-in-trade, the Roadhouse has always offered carryout through the Roadshow, a vintage aluminum trailer that serves as a drive-thru outlet for coffee, pastries, and bread. Diners also could call ahead for items from the breakfast, lunch, and dinner menus. During the governor's original ban on indoor dining, which lasted from March until June 2020, Weinzweig, chef Bob Bennett, and the Roadhouse managers decided to transform the property into a community gathering spot.

Surrounded by parking spaces on all sides, the Roadhouse also has a long strip of lawn out front along Maple Road. There have always been picnic tables, occasionally used by locals for meetings, or by parents for a safe space for little ones to run around. Now that lawn, and the food that customers ordered to eat there, became the Roadhouse's saving grace. As the weather warmed up, Zingerman's installed more brightly colored picnic tables and patio umbrellas. It built a temporary low fence to divide the lawn from the parking lot and added an area where patrons could enjoy drinks from the Roadhouse bar.

For a while, the Roadhouse offered delivery, but Weinzweig discontinued it after a few months. The restaurant's location on the west side of Ann Arbor was too far away from many neighborhoods for food to arrive in decent condition. One afternoon, I ordered fried chicken, only to find that steam inside the box had turned the usually crisp crust into a wilted disappointment. The Roadhouse tried using its own staff for delivery trips, but then faced the cost of car insurance. Meanwhile, Weinzweig was displeased with the 30 percent fees that some delivery companies were charging restaurants.

So, the delivery experiment was discontinued in fall 2020, although the headaches continued. Weinzweig discovered at Christmas that the Postmates delivery company had listed the Roadhouse on its website, even though it had no agreement with Zingerman's to deliver its food. That put the Roadhouse in a bind when a customer called to complain about their order. The Roadhouse didn't have a ticket in that person's name; it was listed with the driver's name, whom the restaurant could not track down.

Meanwhile, the dramatic shift away from being primarily a sit-down restaurant could be seen across the dining rooms. In spring 2021, I was able to take a seat at my favorite front counter once more, although I was now surrounded by Plexiglas save for a small opening where I could chat with the staff. I watched, fascinated, as tray after tray of food came out of the kitchen, with items packed in plastic containers and environmentally friendly clamshell boxes, each labeled with a customer's name. One staff member's sole responsibility was to put the appropriate containers and boxes in brightly colored tote bags, and hand them off to another staff member to run outside to customers waiting in their cars or at the picnic tables.

Before the pandemic, four people handled carryout orders, including those who made coffee drinks inside the aluminum trailer; now, a year into the new system, nine staffers on every shift were responsible for dealing with the takeaway process. Half the front dining room was set aside for carry out supplies and to host a row of constantly ringing phones with customers calling to place orders. The reliance on to-go items also changed the rankings of the Roadhouse's most popular items. The most frequently ordered dish now was a breakfast burrito, which included fluffy scrambled eggs, applewood smoked bacon, melted jack cheese, and green chilies. Who ordered it? I asked a manager, Gaelan Campbell-Fox. "Everybody," he replied. Next came a pulled-pork barbecue sandwich, followed by a classic cheeseburger. Perennial favorites like mac and cheese and the Roadhouse's crispy fried chicken were still in the top ten, but the other dishes, which could be eaten more easily behind the wheel, had elbowed them aside.

Able to welcome guests inside and out, and with a return to events such as special dinners on the horizon, Maurer was optimistic that Roadhouse revenues will climb, too. Although they dropped to $6.5 million for fiscal 2021, from $7.2 million in fiscal 2020, he believed that the Roadhouse would continue gaining for 2022, assuming it could find adequate staff and ingredients. But by fall, 2021, both were becoming major challenges for the busy restaurant. While it had plenty of customers, especially after fans returned to watch football games at the Big House, Weinzweig found himself short on employees and dealing with supply interruptions. Sharon Kramer, a server who had been at the Roadhouse for fourteen years, was so overwhelmed by her growing responsibilities that she tearfully handed in her notice in August 2021. Perennially cheerful and popular with customers and staff alike, Kramer had been instrumental in setting up the restaurant's carryout system, answering phones, organizing boxes with customer orders, and running food to the carryout window, along with waiting on tables. But she felt crushed by the workload, and after weeks of thought, decided to become a manager at a nearby national chain restaurant. "I just wanted a JOB," she told me, not the complexities that she was handling at the Roadhouse.

Yet, Kramer only lasted ten days away. "I'm back home for good!" she declared in an email. She found that her new place fell far short of the quality standards and employee participation to which she'd grown accustomed. She returned to serving Roadhouse guests, setting some boundaries around the amount of additional duties she agreed to take on. Meanwhile, the Roadhouse eliminated some of the innovations it introduced during the pandemic, like service directly to picnic tables, asking that customers walk up to the Roadshow to order instead. It streamlined its food menu, and closed on Tuesdays, a move the restaurant hoped would only be temporary. It was clear that without an end in sight to the pandemic, adjustments would be continuous, echoing the constant improvements that *kaizen* dictated.

CORNMAN FARMS

Cornman lost its 2020 wedding business at its most lucrative time, June through September, costing it about $1 million in revenue during the 2020 fiscal year. When weddings and gatherings could resume, the state limited the number of people who could attend gatherings, robbing it of another $1 million for 2021. The disruption affected both the Cornman staff and the families who had chosen the romantic property for their once-in-a-lifetime events. But adjustments took place on the fly.

In 2019, Cornman had introduced an innovative package called Tiny Weddings, aimed at picking up nontraditional business, like same-sex couples and people who had previously been married and didn't want a lot of fuss. Wedding couples were allowed two hours use of the property, plus a cake and champagne toast, with no more than ten guests (some had none at all). When events were allowed to resume, these packages became so popular that Cornman was conducting as many as five Tiny Weddings a day, with the slots booked months in advance.

Cornman also was able to accommodate slightly bigger groups that still fit within the state's gathering limits. Emma Darvick and Scott Penkava had originally planned on a wedding with ninety guests when they booked Cornman for November 1, 2020. Cutting back their list multiple times, they finally wed with twenty-seven family members and friends in attendance, just below the state's limit at the time of thirty guests. Darvick's mother, Debra, the couple's wedding planner, was determined that the ceremony would go on.

"I wanted to stay with them because I didn't want a business to go out of business. I didn't want to pull whatever we were going to do away from them," she says. While the couple originally planned a simpler menu with small plates, the smaller guest count allowed them to offer a more elaborate meal that included soup, a fall vegetable salad, cheeses, appetizers called gougères, and wine service. Attendees were scattered on different levels of the farmhouse and barn to emphasize social distancing. Cornman's arranged for a Zoom videographer so that absent guests could watch the ceremony.

The original wedding was supposed to cost $30,000, but the smaller one cost $18,000 and Zingerman's even sent a $400 refund once all the expenses were calculated. "I was almost like, 'Don't give it back to me,'" Darvick says. "Knowing it was Zingerman's, I didn't have to worry about anything. I just want to sing their praises everywhere. It was more than lemonade" out of lemons. "It was limoncello." But after eighteen months of sluggish business, Cornman unexpectedly found itself awash in customers in the second half of 2021. People who had delayed holding events now collectively wanted to get back on its calendar. Cornman had always relied on Zingerman's Catering business and the Roadhouse to provide menu items and staff: now, it was leaning on both at a time when employees were hard to find. "It is VERY VERY busy, and unlike a restaurant that can choose to not open a dining room for a shift or reduce their overall restaurant hours, we're in a tough spot because we're contractually obligated to host events," Mason said to me in an August 2021 email. "Tricky, for sure."

VIRTUAL LEARNING

ZingTrain had been tiptoeing into virtual learning when the pandemic hit, but neither Bake! nor the Deli had fully embraced the idea for their classes.

By 2021, all three had shifted to online classes. ZingTrain reinvented its curriculum so that its classes could be offered virtually, and it created new ones geared toward businesses that were struggling in the pandemic. That recouped an estimated $1 million in lost business, according to managing partner Katie Frank, who figured it might return to its $2 million pre-pandemic status by 2023. Maurer says he was impressed by the fast pivot to virtual learning that ZingTrain achieved. "They are amazing," he says, predicting that ZingTrain's revenues eventually could approach $2.7 million by mid-decade.

Meanwhile, Bake! found ways to keep cookbook authors, chefs, and bakers on its events schedule. It taught courses in pretzels, cake, tahini, and even offered a mini pie bake-cation on line. At the Deli, Weinzweig and Singleton teamed up to virtually teach Ari's Favorite Things, while the Deli also set up virtual classes in paella, tea, a chocolate-and-mead pairing, balsamic vinegar, olive oil, and a cheese tasting. In many of the classes, students could purchase ingredients to go along with the instruction, or they could simply pay a fee, sit back, and enjoy what they were learning.

"There's still some work to do to make it really good," Emberling says of the Bake! classes. "It's like a new business, in a way, because you realize there are things you have to communicate. But I think the [virtual] business is definitely sustainable."

CLEANING CLOSETS

Across the organization, the pandemic offered opportunities for the Zingerman's businesses to jettison some of the practices that they had continued simply because it was the way they had operated from the beginning. Emberling likened it to cleaning out a house after the owner had lived there for years. "There's all that stuff that you accumulate in your closet and your drawers that you never clear out. Well, this has sort of forced us to clear out some things, and actually do some things that were on our list and never made it to the top." Adds Carollo, "To lose a tiny bit of the deliberate way that we [operated] and just embrace experiments."

Mangigian immediately saw the opportunity to streamline both the Coffee and Candy operations. These were among the worst hit of the Zingerman's businesses, immediately losing about 80 percent of their revenue. The deepest toll was at Coffee. The independent cafés that Mangigian had carefully cultivated were closed by shutdown orders, while air travel plummeted, devastating Coffee's airport business. Early in the pandemic, Candy closed its retail store, and became a pop-up inside the Coffee shop. The pair eventually recovered some of the lost customers, helped by demand from people working remotely who needed their caffeine fixes to get through the day. By 2021, Mangigian says the two companies were operating at about 50 percent of the revenue they had generated in 2019.

He was plagued by the supply chain delays that were a problem across American businesses, and indeed, were causing global snafus. In one instance, Candy's chocolate supplier in Detroit ran out of ingredients for Zzang bars, forcing Mangigian to track them down in Pennsylvania. His vendor for paper cups and plastic lids used for coffee and tea told him it would take four to five months, rather than the usual few weeks, to send supplies. But Mangigian refused to cut back on the "good service" that Zingerman's promised its customers, vowing that Coffee and Candy would fix its supply problems so that guests weren't short-changed.

The Creamery, next door to Coffee and Candy, also saw a plunge in its business. Arend Elston estimated that revenue dropped two-thirds in the first month of the pandemic and stayed at that lower level for several more months. "We had to lay people off and build back," he says. By August 2021, the Creamery was introducing new products and its mini-Brie was vying with pimiento cheese as its top seller. Down the road, Mangigian was sketching out a plan to knock down the walls between Coffee, Candy, and Creamery and create something like a marketplace, where visitors could shop and eat, making use of outdoor tables as well as socially distanced indoor dining. He envisioned a friendly, open destination that could leverage all the food-producing companies' products.

One shift for all the ZCoB, Emberling says, was from writing annual budgets to crafting quarterly ones. "That's giving us more flexibility," she says. Every two weeks, the managers met to go over lists of what was working and what was not working, and to prepare for upcoming events, like holidays, the shift to cold weather, the shift out of cold weather into spring and summer, and so on. "When you're in a crisis, there's nothing like everybody pulling together," Emberling says. And she's grateful to the Ann Arbor community, as well. "Ann Arbor supports us, and also demands things," she says. "It has standards for us. It's a really productive engagement."

By the 2021 fiscal year, Zingerman's employment had dropped to about 508 people, from 730 when the pandemic began. Once again, regular emails went out, listing the job openings across ZCoB. Maurer says he never lost faith that ZCoB would get through the crisis. "I had supreme confidence that we would be okay," he says. "I was confident we would have the resources to get through it. Did I think every business would make it?" He pauses. "I don't know." Weinzweig says he's proud of the way Zingerman's reacted to a crisis that felled so many restaurants, food shops, and other businesses across the industry. "There's nothing we're not dealing with that anyone else isn't dealing with," he says. "We're a relatively healthy organization that's worked through a lot of stress and duress. It's a little like a veteran team that knows how to win."

CHAPTER FOURTEEN
The Future of Zingerman's

As much as Zingerman's often feels like a family company, it isn't one. There are no heirs waiting to inherit what Weinzweig and Saginaw have created—Saginaw says neither of his adult sons, both musicians, are interested in succeeding him, while Weinzweig doesn't have children. With Saginaw reaching seventy and Weinzweig now sixty-five, it's logical to ask, "What happens to Zingerman's when Ari and Paul are gone?"

The answer is taking shape, prompted by Saginaw's decision in 2020 to launch Saginaw's Deli in Las Vegas. His wife, Lori, jokes that the restaurant is Saginaw's way of retiring from Zingerman's, without actually having to cash out or quit. The contrast between college town and casino mecca might be head-scratching, but Saginaw says that if he hadn't set down roots in Ann Arbor, he could have easily headed for Vegas. In fact, he began going there in his youth. He became interested in gambling through his great-uncle Charles "Chuckie" Sherman, a bookie who was arrested at least sixty-five times, by Saginaw's count. Sherman was swept up in one of Detroit's most famous gambling raids, which took place in May 1971 at the Anchor Bar. More than a hundred and fifty people were arrested, and Sherman was among those charged with running a $40,000 gambling ring. But the charges were dismissed years later when it turned out that the signatures of Justice Department officials on wiretap authorizations were forged.

As a boy, Saginaw accompanied Sherman to local racetracks, where his great-uncle taught him a slide-rule-based system for betting on horses. Then, at twenty-one, he took his first Vegas vacation, and has been going back ever since. "I don't think a year has gone by that I haven't been out there at least once," Saginaw says. In summer 2020, he officially moved west. That October, he opened Saginaw's, a twenty-four-hour deli in the $1 billion Circa Resort & Casino in Vegas's downtown.

Even though he claims that it isn't Zingerman's West, there are plenty of echoes of the original Deli, from the checkered tile floor, to the same philosophy of standout food that powered him and Weinzweig from the beginning. Saginaw brought a flock of Zingerman's staff and friends to help him open, stocked Zingerman's coffee, and he's tried to embrace the Lean techniques that Mail Order has adopted. Unlike the Deli, however, Saginaw's is named for a real person, and in fact, a statue of him sits at the entrance. It also reminded Saginaw of just how hard it can be to run a restaurant. "One day I'm going to stop working and sit down and look back on it," he says of his career. "Now I'm just trying to figure out who'll be lead on the overnight shift."

Saginaw stays involved in Zingerman's daily operations through Zoom calls, emails, and texts, but he doesn't expect to be back in Ann Arbor for the foreseeable future, leaving Weinzweig as the only cofounder on-site.

NOT URGENT UNTIL IT'S URGENT

Saginaw's move prompted Zingerman's to create a four-member stewardship committee, drawn from the managing partners, with two responsibilities. It acts as advisers to Weinzweig in company decisions and has begun work on the structure that Zingerman's might require when both its founders are gone. "It's one of those very important, but 'not urgent until it's urgent' situations," says Singleton. When the committee was formed, Emberling asked Saginaw if he expected to be a member. "Absolutely not," he said. Then he asked Emberling how she felt about that. "I think that you trust us," she replied. "That's exactly what I'm saying," Saginaw replied. "It's your business to run."

Saginaw says the steering committee is a way of "recognizing that Ari and I are eventually going off into the sunset, and you've got to let the next generation of leaders take the helm." Weinzweig, who has no plans to leave anytime soon, does not expect that two people will move up to replace himself and Saginaw. He believes that ZCoB collectively will be overseen by the managing partners, once he and Saginaw have both left, with each business then owned solely by its managing partners. According to a plan Maurer says is in the works, the managing partners would be required to purchase the outstanding percentage of their individual businesses held by Saginaw and Weinzweig when the pair have departed.

But when that transition ultimately happens, Zingerman's could be in the same situation as many other entrepreneurial enterprises. No matter how talented the people that follow, nothing can replace the passion of individual founders, and the experience of having been there at the beginning.

The transition is taking place as Zingerman's customer base changes. Millennials and Generation Z have been born and matured since the company came to life. There are plenty of young people who love dining there, proving that Zingerman's reputation for great food transcends generations. But in the 2020s, fewer customers have personally experienced the old-school deli tradition that drove Weinzweig and Saginaw to open Zingerman's. Tourist favorites like the Carnegie Deli and the Stage Deli in New York are gone, and Manny's, a Chicago favorite, has had to aggressively promote itself on social media to stay in the public eye. Moreover, food trends have changed significantly in the past four decades, notably the shift toward more vegetarian and vegan eating, especially plant-based meat substitutes.

Zingerman's has vegetarian sections on its menus, owns a working farm, and supports fruit and vegetable growers across the area, but its brand is inevitably tied up with animal products—bacon, beef, and poultry, as well as the dairy products made by the Creamery and used across ZCoB.

Meanwhile, there is an avid market for the driveway pop-ups and other events that flourished across Ann Arbor and the Detroit area during the pandemic. The owners of these temporary kitchens shine on social media, with handles like Basil Babe, Detroit Brad, Luecha Puerco, and of course, Chef G, who brought his stand to the Creamery. One small business, Side Biscuit, was opened in 2021 by Jordan Balduf, a veteran of several Zingerman's kitchens. Many of these young entrepreneurs would seem like prime candidates to become managers at Zingerman's establishments and possibly aim for a managing partnership down the road. They have the enthusiastic backing of Ji Hye Kim, a veteran of the Roadhouse kitchen whose food truck and Miss Kim restaurant were launched by Zingerman's.

But for now, at least, this culinary generation has discovered the freedom (and headaches) of working for themselves, at events a couple of nights a week at places like York Yard, Cultivate Coffee and Tap House in nearby Ypsilanti, even if they can't promise the smoothness and customer service of a Zingerman's business. In March 2021, Balduf, a native of Buffalo, opened a brick-and-mortar version of the pop-up that he operated at York, a beer-and-wine store whose cofounder, Tommy York, was briefly a managing partner at the Deli.

Within days, Balduf was managing his own version of the Line, which stretched down the street. He frequently sold out of multiple flavors of chicken wings in a few hours each night, attracting an enthusiastic following, although soaring wholesale costs prompted him to bump up his menu prices. Balduf speaks enthusiastically about the training he got at Zingerman's, and remains a Friend of Zingerman's. By going out on his own, however, he didn't have to wait the eighteen months that it would have taken to complete the path to becoming a Zingerman's managing partner, and he could create his own brand. Nor did he need Saginaw and Weinzweig to finance his operations: He found a backer in Cultivate owner Sara Demorest. While he was waiting to open his business, he held a series of pop-ups across the area, and recouped his $20,000 investment in Side Biscuit before he even opened.

In its vision for 2032, which follows this chapter, Zingerman's speaks of operating fifteen to twenty businesses, including those that do not sell food. These pop-up entrepreneurs sound exactly like the kind of passionate people that the company would love to attract, and Saginaw believes they would benefit from the education that Zingerman's can give them. Certainly, there's plenty to be said for the experience that an establishment like Zingerman's can provide, along with its resources. In 2021, I attended a Fourth of July pop-up whose trio of young chefs were overwhelmed by more than five hundred orders. After waiting almost an hour for my food, I gave in to the summer heat and humidity that were making me feel dizzy, leaving my order behind. With the staff so busy trying to keep up, there was no one to ask for a refund and no one to check on how I was doing during the long delay.

Meanwhile, several of the young chefs confided to me that they were looking at options beyond pop-ups that might reduce the stress they were feeling. Like restaurants, they were constantly searching to find people to work their gigs. They also were encountering the same rising food prices and shortages of ingredients that restaurants were battling. Maybe, they admitted, there was something to be said about a brick-and-mortar place like the Deli or the Roadhouse, and working just eight hours a night. Saginaw, looking at the chefs' situation from the forty-year perspective of running the Deli, said that a food career was a learning process.

"Partners don't come in as finished products," Saginaw says, and the path they must travel teaches them some vital business tools. But, Zingerman's has been learning what it needs in partners, too. In its first couple of decades, its expansion often took place because someone who worked there wanted to produce something—coffee, candy, cheese—regardless of whether there was a distinct market for it, or a good business case to be made. Yet, as Saginaw admits, that created a collection of businesses where some are wildly successful, and others are barely staying afloat, contrary to his goal that all of them be sustainable.

Despite his belief that there's more to business than just making money, he agrees that Zingerman's future will rest in part on its financial viability. In order to grow, it has to produce the good finances that the company talks about as one of its three bottom lines. That's a reason why people who gained business experience elsewhere, from Chicago, to Frankenmuth, Michigan, and Boston, are among the partners and those on the partnership path.

"We imagined this company back in 1994," Saginaw says of ZCoB. "The initial vision was that we would have these little cottage businesses. We never imagined we would have these large ones. The structure is not doing justice to who we are." He believes that there's room for Zingerman's to become more efficient without affecting its corporate culture. Given the warm response Saginaw received when he sought possible rescue funding in 2020, it's clear that investors would be interested in purchasing pieces of Zingerman's, if not acquiring the brand outright, as has happened with so many food companies that have sold to private equity. Financial experts who admire the company say its brand is enormously valuable, perhaps worth as much as $1 billion, if the Zingerman's name could be leveraged across the country. That might seem eye-popping, given that Zingerman's annual revenue is below $100 million. But San Francisco's beloved Blue Bottle Coffee began with a single coffee cart in 2002, two decades after the Deli, and was purchased by Nestlé in 2017 for a reported $700 million.

Saginaw is skeptical of investors' back-of-the-envelope projections, however. "We don't pay attention to that," he says of the valuation estimates, "because it's not what we're going to do." However, there could be an opportunity for the public to buy into Zingerman's at some point. For the past few years, Maurer, Saginaw, and Weinzweig have discussed creating a separate entity that could sell shares or some sort of ownership stake to investors, based on Zingerman's intellectual property. Investments would be at risk, and payouts would depend on how well ZCoB performs. Maurer says that plan continues to take shape and is confident "there will be a way that people can buy into the ZCoB," he says.

However, Saginaw is emphatic that the system of individual businesses, run by managing partners, is crucial to Zingerman's future. "How we're structured is not unconnected to who we are, and the success that we've realized," he says. To be blunt, if somebody tries to take Zingerman's apart, or build it into something too big, they might wind up ruining the whole enterprise in the process. He has a good point. In *Start with Why*, Simon Sinek says none of a company's relationships—between managers and staff, and with customers—can be nurtured without a feeling of camaraderie. "Trust begins to emerge when we have a sense that another person or organization is driven by things other than their own self-gain," he writes.

Listening to Saginaw, I was reminded of the peonies that bloom in Ann Arbor gardens each spring, a welcome sight after months of gray skies and snow. The farmer's market overflows with luscious, fragrant flowers in white, pink, fuchsia, and deep red, and thousands of visitors descend on the Nichols Arboretum, near the University of Michigan Medical Center, to stroll among the colorful bushes. I've always been fascinated by watching the tight, round buds begin to unfurl, expand, and reach their peak glory in size and scent. But, as every gardener knows, once peonies reach that point, they can suddenly disintegrate. Simply jostle them, and their beautiful petals flutter to the floor.

As Zingerman's heads into its fifth decade, its future seems to echo that of those stunning peonies. Everything it has accomplished in its first forty years adds up to a company that is widely admired for its food, its customer service, and the business philosophy it has shared across the landscape. But its structure sometimes seems as fragile as a full-blown peony. A team of MBAs could descend on Zingerman's and find countless ways to extend the brand and yield more profit. However, those conventional improvements might have the same result as disturbing a bouquet, ruining the essence of what has made the company so admired. Abra Berens, for one, thinks it would be a mistake to disrupt the "deliberate inefficiencies" that she spotted during her years at the Deli. "Working at Zingerman's ruined me for any other employment," she says. "That constant striving for excellence is a pretty good problem to have."

You might enjoy a Reuben, appreciate the information that a cheese monger gives you, and applaud a passing Food Gatherers truck. But Zingerman's is a mosaic of everything you've read in this book. You don't get a full picture of the company until you see how all of its pieces fit together.

Zingerman's was born and grew at a time when Americans were deeply curious about food, interested in tasting flavors from the past and exploring cuisines that were less familiar. The company also lucked out enormously by being based in a wealthy community with plenty of discretionary income and a willingness to spend money on food. Zingerman's, to those who love it, not only feeds the body, but fuels the self as well, in the customers who leave smiling and the employees who enjoy their jobs. In the darkest days of the pandemic, and the uncertain times that persist, Zingerman's has not just been a Community of Businesses; it has been a community with its customers.

Whether buying a loaf of bread, tearing it open to eat with cheese, or learning to make that bread, Zingerman's customers usually feel a sense of appreciation. During the pandemic, they considered the company a link to a life they temporarily could not lead, even if the baked goods cost tens of dollars more than a babka or a coffeecake elsewhere. That's the kind of loyalty businesses crave—and which steers them through challenges. Says Frank Carollo, "I've done something that I've felt strongly about and proud of every day that I've ever worked. When we started, we didn't think about being a brand. We thought about making something really, really great that people would want."

EMPHASIZING JOY

But beyond its food, Zingerman's has had an indelible impact on the way people who come in contact with it think and feel. In 2015, long before anyone anticipated the woes that the pandemic might trigger, Weinzweig and Saginaw stood on a platform inside Michigan Stadium, known as the Big House. Decades after their own graduations, the two UM alumni were there to receive honorary doctor-of-laws degrees, part of a distinguished group that include the journalist Robin Wright, who grew up in Ann Arbor, and John D. Dingell Jr., the irascible Michigan lawmaker who became the longest-serving member of Congress.

As laid-back as they might have appeared to the vast crowd, they were both nervous. Weinzweig hadn't attended any of his own graduation ceremonies, and despite his experience in speaking to all sizes of crowds, he'd never seen anything like the fifty thousand people who had gathered at the Big House ceremony. Meanwhile, before the speech, Saginaw spotted a comment online that read, "Wow, whoever was the first choice must have backed out!" He admits he wondered if that was true. In preparation, the pair decided to split up the speaking duties: Weinzweig was focused on talking about moral beliefs, which he had been writing about, while Saginaw wanted to impart useful, but not clichéd, advice.

For weeks before the address, Saginaw practiced his part of the speech with his wife, Lori, paragraph by paragraph. Only when he felt satisfied with a paragraph did he move on to polishing the next. Weinzweig was the opposite. He shied away from rehearsing because he wanted to sound more spontaneous. "I don't like giving a fifteen-minute scripted speech," he says. "I don't like hearing the sound of my voice."

Once they got onstage, the men discovered there was a lengthy lag between what they said, and the reply from the crowd, which they each found a little unnerving. But after an initial wave of laughter reached them across the massive stadium, the pair began to find their rhythm and gave what NPR ranked among "the Best Commencement Speeches, Ever."

Saginaw asked the students to pull up their mental to-do lists for their post-graduation life, and to see whether "joy" was at the top. If it wasn't, he advised them to include it. "Joy is a feeling so profound that it sits at the top of the human experience chart," he told the graduates and their families. "To feel joy, you don't have to wait until you're old, like us, I believe you can have it now, starting today. How? Generosity. Generosity leads to joy. It's simple, and it's guaranteed."

Added Weinzweig, "I believe that perhaps the hardest work we have to undertake is the work no one else sees, and that no else can ever do for us. It's the lifelong challenge to manage ourselves effectively, to make peace with ourselves, and turn our natural ability into a positive and powerful presence in the world."

Speaking in turn, the pair ended by saying to the graduates, "Be generous! Be joyful! Be great! Make a difference!"

There is no doubt that Zingerman's has.

Zingerman's Vision for 2032

Just as Michigan ordered businesses to shut down in the wake of the COVID-19 pandemic, Zingerman's was completing its vision for 2032, when it will mark a half century in business. As you've learned in the book, visions are guiding documents that paint a picture of where Zingerman's hopes to be at a future date. While it's rare for Zingerman's to hit every note in a vision, its previous ones provide a pretty accurate picture of what the company has become. A key component of a vision is for Zingerman's to share it with employees, so they can understand the company's priorities and know why decisions get made.

Very few companies provide employees or the public with this kind of thinking so many years in advance. Some might talk about the coming year or announce their goals for a few years hence. One exception is Toyota. Around 2005, I sat through a presentation that looked at where the company expected to be in 2010, 2020, and 2030. Interestingly, its 2030 forecast predicted that automobiles would no longer be powered exclusively by internal combustion engines (those that use gasoline). That might wind up being a few years sooner than reality, but a number of nations have announced plans to ban gasoline-powered cars in 2035 or 2040, so Toyota has been on track for that eventuality.

With that in mind, let's look at Zingerman's vision for 2032, written by its Visioning Committee in 2020. (I've provided some context where needed.)

ZINGERMAN'S 2032 VISION

It's our fiftieth year! That's right. The Big 5-O! And the Zingerman's Community of Businesses is healthier, happier, and more financially sound than ever. We have continued to break creative ground in the world of progressive business, service, food, work experiences, love, and care. In an era where electronic interaction is now the norm, our personalized, passion-driven, person-to-person connections set us further apart from the mainstream.

As we have for nearly forty years now, since the 2009 vision was written in 1994, we operate as one coherent organizational community, honoring the fifteen to twenty Zingerman's businesses that are a part of it. All are located here in the Ann Arbor area. Some of the businesses are "big," others are small. All strive for excellence in their respective areas of expertise. Each business in the ZCoB has a managing partner or partners who own real shares in the business, have a deep passion for what that business does, and are charged with leading its work.

1. **Food That's More Flavorful Than Ever, and a Host of Other Super-Fine Stuff!**

    Great food is how we started and it still drives us today. Zingerman's has been connecting folks with great food since 1982. We love how much the entire Ann Arbor area food community has grown over the years—we're happily part of a very healthy culinary ecosystem.

    Every dish we serve is fantastic. We've achieved this, in part, because we've never stopped asking, "How can it be better?" Flavor is consistently fuller, finishes are longer, complexity of flavor has been taken to new heights. The Great Food Group led the way to define our ZCoB-wide food philosophy, and each business in the ZCoB has found a way to make it their own. It starts with traditional and full-flavored, and gets much more detailed from there. We use our documented philosophy to evaluate each product and recipe. Is it full-flavored, traditional, local, does it have a known identity, "clean," sustainable, profitable, healthy, differentiating, fun, service to the guest, and so on? Our choices are super intentional.

We started systematically questioning every choice we were making in our recipes and products from the big stuff down to the smallest details. We pushed aside our limiting beliefs and did what everyone says isn't possible. Are these the best onions? Is this the best butter to serve with our bread? How's the ketchup? When is it the right choice to make an item for ourselves? We found more flavorful options and we chose them. Then, with the ingredients in place, there's the precision and skill in making our food. Our systems and training are working to effectively reduce waste in its eight different forms. Lean kitchens, we are!

History comes alive every day in our food. While much of the food world follows the trends, changing focus every five or six months, we are still committed to rediscovering and educating about traditional, full-flavored foods. We are the experts people call for advice about ingredients, recipes, products, and food prep. We've been known for our historical approach and it continues. We've uncovered foods we never thought existed. Old-school sources—little known or understood outside their home regions—are now standards of ZCoB fare.

We've engaged more deeply with our geographic roots and our initial identity as a Jewish deli.

We've initiated the creation of the Great Lakes Foodways Alliance. *(Note: This does not yet exist.)* It's on its way to becoming a nationally recognized nonprofit organization to study foodways, culture, and promote engagement with diverse cultures and cooking styles. It's enabled us to share many of the traditions of the Midwest, rarely understood in the mainstream food world. The really wild rice of the Ojibwe people, corn dogs, the African American farming tradition, Wisconsin cheese, Detroit Coney Island (hot dogs), and Detroit-style pizza to name a few.

What else is at the core of our identity? Great Jewish food. It's still a critical differentiator for many of the ZCoB businesses. Originally we were focused on Ashkenazi Jewish food. Now the cuisines of Jews from the Magreb, South America, and India to name a few places in the Jewish Diaspora, are served and sold throughout the ZCoB. The variety and breadth is remarkable.

We teach the public what we do to make and sell food—baking, cooking, cheese making, coffee tasting, and loads more. People from all over come to learn the skills and techniques that underlie our craft. There's so much going on that Food Tours has six week-long ZCoB tours sold out each year. Guests are tasting, dining, learning, and making in all of our businesses. They're having a blast while they're doing it. They leave very full with more food for home, memories, and our many cookbooks.

2. **Service That Makes You Smile**

Albert Schweitzer said, "The only ones among you who will be truly happy are those who will have sought and found how to serve." We are truly happy. Each of us recognizes that our work here is more meaningful because of the service we give to our guests and to each other.

The Zingerman's Experience in 2032 is as enriching and amazing as it was at Zingerman's Deli in 1982. We set the bar for service then and we are still setting the bar today. Great service happens everywhere: Each element of Zingerman's is a marvelous experience. We are as connected, selfless, and accurate in our opening acts of hospitality with a guest as we are when we recover from a problem. The 3 Steps and the 5 Steps in their simple elegance live on and are serving us well. Our customers, our suppliers, our community, our fellow employees—everyone considers Zingerman's the definition of great service.

While other businesses are using technology to offer fast and easy transactions with little human contact, we are finding ways to use technology to provide the Zingerman's Experience. Our guests feel seen, known and heard while still receiving easy and speedy service. Small considerations, small courtesies, and small kindnesses habitually practiced, day in and day out, build the experience of great service in our many different business contexts. We make meaningful differences in people's lives, one interaction at a time.

Customization and flexibility are setting us apart. We create spaces and service that honors people's needs in regard to dietary needs and choices. We are a favorite place to shop for customers with a variety of personal challenges from life-stage considerations like having young children with them while shopping to being elderly and using a walker. We are known as good places to shop for people living with physical disabilities. We are well aware of the ever-evolving social norms in our community and provide service with sensitivity that reflects this knowledge. We are well known for our staff's empathy and attention to detail when helping people. We engage with each person, open-minded, ready to serve them as they would like, honoring their uniqueness.

We are well aware that we can only give as good service to guests as we receive from each other. Internal service is foundational to our success. Servant leadership is lived and taught at all levels of the organization. Our Managing Partners, Managers, Supervisors, Shift Leads, and Staff all actively recognize the role they play in creating a culture of great service in the workplace. We have set up systems and events which support positive internal culture and recognition. Compassion and connection radiate across the flow of each day and shine through in our staff feedback.

3. **Sustainable Finance: It's About Health, Not About Wealth**

Before we moved into opening any new businesses, we were intentional to focus inside, making the Zingerman's businesses financially healthy across a range of measures, from profitability to cash to debt. We've stayed that way ever since. As part of that we developed—and still use—a robust system of engaging with each other about finances that is objective and out in the open. It's like spellcheck for finances—when a business starts to show trouble signs in its operating numbers, this system kicks in to provide support. We wonder how we lived without it for so long.

What's changed in the last twelve years? We've made it possible for new start-ups to be nimble, tailoring our techniques to be good for bootstraps, while at the same time thriving as a mature organization that's hitting the half-a-century mark! The results are all around us. We have balanced growth across the ZCoB. Mature businesses and start-ups, producers and sellers—all work together to make a diverse, financially sound organization. Financial institutions fight for our business. We're in a strong cash position so we can self-finance ventures when it makes sense and manage the rainy days when they come. There are more opportunities for promotion and partnership than ever before.

There are now Zingerman's businesses that don't make or sell food. ZingTrain was the first, but now there are others. Like our food businesses, they make artisan products or offer services at a very high level of quality. This has given our loyal customers even more ways to enjoy the Zingerman's Experience, allowing us to enhance the diversity of our ecosystem for greater organizational health. Each new business enhances the whole of the ZCoB in a sustainable, dynamic way. This has also opened up new avenues for ZCoBbers who want to be managing partners here to pursue their passions by starting new Zingerman's businesses.

One of those ZCoB businesses, which we started sometime in the 2020s after we'd become financially stable, was one that invests—relatively small at first—amounts of money in values-aligned, non-Zingerman's businesses that we want to support and be involved in, but not own or manage. This work connects us with socially conscious activities that allow us to be supportive of folks who aren't in the ZCoB but we care about; and allows the ZCoB to benefit from those businesses' knowledge and their profitability.

4. **Great Place to Work: Bring Our Whole Selves to Work**

The sense of being seen, welcomed, and appreciated starts on day one in the ZCoB. We help new staff feel included more effectively and quickly than ever. Every person experiences from all others an acceptance and a rightful sense of belonging. We have achieved a level of trust in our organization that enables individuals to be able to speak frankly and be confident that their contribution will be heard, acknowledged, and valued.

We feel honored and humbled that so many great people continue to choose to work at Zingerman's. Our environment supports personal and professional growth. Leaders in the organization are committed to helping each person who works here to be themselves in their own unique way in the world. We teach Visioning as an integral leadership and life skill that's amazingly embedded in the ZCoB systems and culture. We support this process of development and self-discovery wherever it leads, whether that means folks make a career here or work with us for just a bit and move on to pursue their dreams elsewhere.

The work environment in the ZCoB is thriving, and every corner of the organization is connected, engaged, and creative. Our systems allow for flexibility, opportunity, and carving one's own path. More ZCoBbers than ever are working shifts across business and department lines, facilitating the exchange of ideas and dynamically moving resources to where they are most needed.

Our thriving culture is supported by a compensation package that leads our respective industries and stages of business development. We've figured out creative ways to pay more, charge more where we need to, use continuous improvement to cut costs where we can, and end up with healthy profits in the process. We're showing the world that one can pay more and make more money! We design our benefits programs intentionally and use business resources in ways that are truly meaningful to staff and their families.

We creatively found a way to sell food at cost to every Zingerman's employee. The regularly offered ingredient marketplace pop-ups are extremely popular with ZCoBbers all around! Making our products and sources more accessible to our staff makes it easier to know our food deeply: what it tastes like, where it came from, and how to use it. People come to work with us knowing that life will taste better and feel better. Our workplace is notably healthier than ever—physically, mentally, and spiritually.

5. **Community Roots: Staying Put in Order to Grow**

Our dedication to the Ann Arbor area is a huge piece of what makes us who we are. It challenges us to stay close, it excites us, it makes us creative. It's a powerful and paradoxical paradigm. By choosing to stay local we have opened up opportunities we never imagined. We understand the wisdom of Zen poet Gary Snyder's words, "First, don't move; and second, find out what that teaches you."

We have become the community organization we always hoped to be. We know the people in the Ann Arbor area and serve them ever more personally. This dedication to working in the community in which we began is a big piece of what continues to draw attention to us and make us special. People visit us not only for the food and service, but also because they can't get the unique combination of what we do anywhere else. We sell our food across America. But the Zingerman's Experience, delivered in full and in person, is available nowhere else.

We have strong connections with community groups across the area, from churches to senior centers, mosques to book clubs, synagogues to sports teams, hospitals to high schools. All kinds of groups who might not have thought about being connected to Zingerman's are part of our fabric. We looked honestly at ourselves and who we were serving and who did not feel connected to us. We asked why and how we could be appealing to more of our community and how to effectively engage with people. The result is deeper and broader-spread roots throughout our community. It feels great and sales have increased, too. Generosity, it turns out, is a solid business practice.

Zingerman's is a point of pride for our neighbors: the place "everyone" brings out-of-town guests; that job recruiters come to show off with great regularity; that people choose to invest in; that people choose to work for. We continue to find creative ways to surprise and delight our guests, whether it's their first time at Zingerman's or they've known us since they were kids. Showing "love and care" in all our actions is part of our mission—and it's more than what we do, it's who we are.

6. **Working with Young People**

Treating young people and children as valued customers has been core to how we give great service since the beginning. In the past decade, we have connected with the younger members of our community in new ways by developing and offering learning opportunities especially for them. We teach about food, Visioning, finance, leadership, and more. Staff members also love being able to share this Zingerman's Experience with their own families.

Our philosophies and organizational recipes are taught from grade school to grad school. We have strong ties with half a dozen local schools, including the colleges and culinary schools that surround us. Each ZCoB business developed its own ways of being involved with kids, and together we've created new approaches to teaching. For students, this work allows them to experience these ideas in practice every day. We are not just telling stories; we are actively working alongside them and learning together! We have incorporated what we've learned from these young people into our organization. We value their ideas, their creativity, their palates. This work has deepened our own beliefs about the importance of inclusion and treating everyone with dignity and generosity.

Many of the local learners have come to work in the ZCoB and build on opportunities right here. Even more are putting their studies and practices to work as they head to college or out into the world at large. Kids like to vision, they instinctively understand Open Book Management, they thrive on appreciations, they lead change. They can learn to think freely, pursuing their own passions while respecting those of their peers. Kids can run their own classrooms, start businesses and not-for-profits. It's energizing and inspiring to see young people actualizing their visions. We feel honored to have played a part in assisting them along their paths.

7.   **Diversity, Equity, and Inclusion**

We are closer by all measurements to becoming an antiracist organization with diversity, equity, inclusion, and compassion at our core. We continue to seek advice from skilled DEI professionals outside our organization, and every business participates in its own way. We prioritize diversity by systematically and incrementally increasing the number of recruits, hires, and promotions of candidates of color and candidates from a wide variety of socioeconomic and educational backgrounds. We value above experience a candidate's desire to learn and receive training. We practice "calling in" (rather than calling out) each other when we encounter or sense the invisible manifestations of white supremacy with a specific protocol that is taught to everyone.

We prioritize equity by replacing monolithic policies with those that can be and are regularly adapted to meet individual needs and abilities in order to optimize every person's success. Permission to practice this is given to all employees. We regularly share with each other the creative ways in which we have adapted policies in this manner so learning is continuous and widespread. We understand the tricky relationship of impact and intent, acknowledging that harmful impact is not reduced or excused by good intention.

We prioritize inclusivity by giving leadership responsibilities and roles to those whose identities differ from the historic Zingerman's leadership profiles. We have a class to learn and practice dialogue with each other to increase understanding of all points of view. We learn and practice productive ways to address implicit biases and we share our successes in unlearning biases. Throughout the organization we consistently seek out and listen to the voices and ideas of people of color and those of other nonmainstream identities, ensuring that as many perspectives as possible are always at the decision-making table. We make an effort to habitually acknowledge and appreciate learning from one another.

We believe that we have a legal, moral, and ethical obligation to take risks if we want to change the game. This meant that over ten years ago, we radically changed our recruiting methods to actively search out different populations to apply for opportunities in the ZCoB. We measured the results of our efforts in a quantifiable way. We took those initial steps, and we created a policy-driven approach to guide us in our work. Our guide is a living document, and people are using it in their day-to-day work. We regularly evaluate our hiring practices, classes, and the methods we use to train our managers. We have systematized a feedback loop to continue to address and drive out unconscious bias. We adjusted our application process to create a culture of equity. This culture guides us in all of our programming, processes, policies, and decision making so that our practices are in alignment with our vision. When there is an opportunity for advancement in our organization, the path is clear, equitable, and objective. We have knocked down barriers in our systems and culture to allow for all levels of staff to participate in the 1+1 activities that enrich personal work experiences and benefit the ZCoB as a whole.

We have an expectation that everyone in our organization acts with the belief that we are richer in creative resources and energies because we function as a team of people from all backgrounds, orientations, and experiences. We use every opportunity to show appreciation and respect toward one another. We reject the domination of white patriarchal beliefs, and when invisible or subconscious signs of it show up, we help each in a caring way to recognize it and address it.

Our daily efforts to prioritize diversity, equity, inclusivity, and compassion in our workplace have become part of our image as a business, have lowered turnover and raised productivity and creativity, have attracted new customers and increased sales, and have brought us closer to being the company we aspire to be.

8. **How We Work: Collaboration and Autonomy, Freedom and Accountability**

We embrace the seemingly paradoxical principles of autonomy and collaboration. Each business in the ZCoB feels the benefit of being part of the whole while experiencing the freedom of being an individual. As a Community of Businesses, we truly are stronger together than we are apart. We value the knowledge and experience of our colleagues across department lines, business lines, in all levels of the organization. We have improved our communication methods as we have grown so that information flows throughout the organization seamlessly. Together, we seek out solutions that provide the most benefit to the largest contingent of our organization. When choosing between a path that is best for one of our businesses, or one that is great for multiple businesses, we select the option that shares the positive impact among many.

We've defined this synergy and made it visible: tracking it at ZCoB huddles and building it into ZAP goals. These metrics have made it much easier to see how helping each other makes a difference. We actively teach and use the Collaboration Compact, which gives us a clear set of expectations and guidelines on how to do this work well. As a ZCoB, we regularly evaluate our organizational blind spots and make strategic plans to fill the gaps. We identify skill sets and functions that can benefit the whole, and we have found ways to put resources behind those efforts, leading to meaningful impact.

Success starts with each of us. We hold ourselves accountable for our own commitments. We also respectfully hold each other accountable by asking questions, providing feedback, and agreeing up front on rewards and creative consequences. We think of holding each other accountable as an act of service. We don't place blame; we offer to help. We acknowledge that no matter where we are in our career paths, we are all continually learning and developing as individuals.

9. **Moving at the Speed of Yes: Reflection and Action**

We keep our minds open to innovation. We champion a creative culture of possibility and invention. When someone shares a new idea, we ask, "How can we make that work here?" We engage in creative thinking and open communication to explore those ideas. We ask questions, seeking to understand. We learn and grow with eyes and hearts open. We lean toward freedom and experimentation. It's a delicate balance—stewardship of past practices and agreements and embracing new approaches. We are intentional about our decisions to change, and actively choose when it is best to stay the course. We are quick to engage in low-risk innovation opportunities that fit within the framework of our Mission, Vision, and Guiding Principles. Sometimes we take big risks, knowing that our organization is strong, resilient, and that the risk of potential failure will not be catastrophic.

ZCoB partners and leaders are practiced in the art of Followership. As Sir Kenneth Robinson said, "The role of a creative leader is not to have all the ideas; it's to create a culture where everyone can have ideas and feel they're valued." We believe that the people doing the work are the best equipped to make recommendations for improving that work. We all have both the opportunity and the responsibility to shape the organization that we want. Leading change at Zingerman's is a rewarding process that is accessible to everyone here.

We have established an Experiential Learning Lab and we teach its systems in Basic Orientation. We believe that hands-on learning by trying things out will illuminate solutions. We have seen how incremental changes create forward momentum. We approach everything we do in the spirit of learning and continuous improvement. This style of going for greatness has been put into practice in all facets of our work, from food to finance, from service improvements to internal operations.

10. **Walking New Paths: Succession and Continuity**

Over the last twelve years we've seen a successful transition from Ari and Paul as founders heading the ZCoB to a mode of governance that will last beyond the tenure of any individual. While longtime ZCoB leaders continue in important roles, a couple of new "generations" of insightful, collaborative folks have stepped forward. Past partners are still involved and helping to guide us. The ZCoB has grown stronger through that transition.

Organizational governance processes are clear. We embrace the challenge of building freedom for all while holding ourselves coherently and caringly together. We cultivate decisions, getting people on board, and when we are all excited and behind an idea, it's palpable. We have chosen decision-making tools to balance leadership, followership, speed, and business need. We built this model with the belief that power and ownership should be shared, not hoarded.

Ownership is now spread more deeply and widely throughout the organization and into our community. Half our staff own Community Shares. Community Share Owners are more involved than ever in leading the ZCoB. In addition to their daily duties, they're teachers, leaders, systems designers, and culture builders who enhance the collective wisdom of Zingerman's. We added a second type of shares in our "brand"—Legacy Shares—which has provided another avenue for investing in the organization with all of the ups (and at times, some downs) of stock ownership. Many businesses have figured out their own forms of staff ownership as well.

11. **Working in Harmony with Nature**

We've successfully adopted a model of sustainability to all aspects of our work. A Guiding Principle of Sustainability describes the culture of our work that is economically viable, socially responsible, and ecologically sound. We work to harmonize the many parts of our organizational ecosystem; people and place, the planet and our processes come together and all are better for the collaboration. Everyone and everything we engage with—in our personal and professional lives; our business and community; our customers and staff; our suppliers and environment—are working in harmony with nature. Whether it's gardens supporting our businesses; the traffic flow in our businesses; the way we organize meetings, design processes and job descriptions; how we create organizational structures, explore creativity, etc., we design with natural, sustainable systems in mind. All of our businesses across the ZCoB have taken to heart the Lean principle of waste reduction. Every business has found ways to both use less and create less waste in our production and service. Ninety-five percent of what we have left over is either upcycled, recycled, or composted.

We had to take a hard look at how we're moving around the city, and why we're doing it. Cars and travel, in 2020, were making up 40 percent of emissions in our city. What we found, though, was that we could travel in ways that are healthier, and build a better community than we ever could have thought. The impact was huge on the ZCoB. After we started tracking our mileage, we found that we have reduced our single-person miles driven in cars by 40 percent, really helping to support the city. We also came up with more efficient routes for deliveries, and we've completely electrified our fleet of delivery vehicles.

We are stewards of—and also a part of—the planet. When we source each ingredient we use, we aim to make thoughtful and purposeful choices, keeping environmental sustainability, energy usage, and ethics in mind. We continue to find that great taste is connected to and reflective of the care the producer takes in producing their products. We consider the production methods of the products we use and sell. Our support and featuring of these products have helped highlight the benefits of sustainable and regenerative production methods. We have found ways to support working this way, knowing it may cost us more financially at the outset. We have found ways to balance and offset these costs by streamlining each area of our work, rarely needing to raise our prices in an effort to support our sustainability goals. Our customers care about being connected to this work we are doing, and we actively share our learnings with them.

There are improvements we have made that we couldn't have imagined back when we wrote this vision, in so many ways, large and small. We are flexible, creative, and responsive. With the lead of Planet Zing, we work each day with these key factors in mind: Food Choices, Our Waste Stream, Responsible Packaging, Lean Culture, and Facilities Management. We measure our energy production each month in each business. We have gone beyond Net Zero—we are Net Positive.

12. Love and Care

Every act in the ZCoB is an act of love. Acts to care and connect. To take the implementation of our mission to greater heights than ever. We view everyone through the lens of a compassionate heart, choosing patience and positive beliefs, and take pause to appreciate the beauty in everyone and everything we work with. We are mindfully conscious of what the impact of our decisions is on the people we work with, our customers, and the larger community. We understand that the energy we put into every interaction is essential. We are self-reflective and intentional in our work in this way.

Compassion is a deep understanding of the feelings and experiences of others. Working in this way allows us to demonstrate care, and genuine care for others creates real connections. It makes us authentic. These authentic connections create trust, cooperation, and eagerness/willingness to work together. We lead with compassion.

How does this look if disagreements or frustrations arise today? We engage and interact with each other to come from a place of love, knowing that welcoming the discomfort can be the key to our growth and better understanding of each other and ourselves. We first assume positive intent in our engagement. We have caring interactions even when we disagree—feeling heard and having courageous conversations without contempt. We work to change our beliefs to see how people change and grow, supporting them on their path. We share this journey together.

> We share the Zingerman's Experience
> Selling food that makes you happy
> Giving service that makes you smile
> In passionate pursuit of our mission
> Showing love and care in all our actions
> To enrich as many lives as we possibly can.

Appendix

A Brief Zingerman's Timeline

1982: Zingerman's Deli opens in the Kerrytown section of Ann Arbor.

1988: Zingerman's launches Food Gatherers, Michigan's first food rescue program.

1992: Zingerman's Bakehouse opens in an industrial park that will become Zingerman's South Side.

1993: The first Mail Order catalog is published.

1994: ZingTrain launches; Zingerman's Community of Businesses is formed; Zingerman's first Vision is published.

1996: Zingerman's Catering opens; Zingerman's Mail Order is founded.

1997: Zingerman's Food Tours launches.

1999: Zingermans.com goes live.

2001: Zingerman's Creamery opens in Manchester, Michigan (it later moves to Ann Arbor); Zingerman's announces plans to put a Deli in Detroit Metropolitan Airport. It is canceled after the 9/11 attacks.

2003: Zingerman's Roadhouse, the first sit-down restaurant, opens on the west side of Ann Arbor; Zingerman's Coffee Company is founded inside Mail Order; it moves to Zingerman's South Side.

2009: Zingerman's Candy Manufactory opens at Zingerman's South Side.

2014: Zingerman's acquires Cornman Farms in Dexter, Michigan.

2016: Miss Kim opens in Kerrytown; Greyline, an events space, opens in downtown Ann Arbor.

W. Edwards Deming's 14 Points

1. Create constancy of purpose for improving products and services.
2. Adopt the new philosophy.
3. Cease dependence on inspection to achieve quality.
4. End the practice of awarding business on price alone; instead, minimize total cost by working with a single supplier.
5. Improve constantly and forever every process for planning, production, and service.
6. Institute training on the job.
7. Adopt and institute leadership.
8. Drive out fear.
9. Break down barriers between staff areas.
10. Eliminate slogans, exhortations, and targets for the workforce.
11. Eliminate numerical quotas for the workforce and numerical goals for management.
12. Remove barriers that rob people of pride of workmanship, and eliminate the annual rating or merit system.
13. Institute a vigorous program of education and self-improvement for everyone.
14. Put everybody in the company to work accomplishing the transformation.

Bibliography

If you're interested in exploring Zingerman's management concepts, its approach to service, or learning more about its food, Zingerman's offers a variety of books that delve deeply into those topics. Here is an assortment that I'd recommend, along with two other titles.

FOOD

Zingerman's Guide to Good Eating, Ari Weinzweig, 2003 (Rux Martin/ Houghton Mifflin Harcourt)

Zingerman's Bakehouse, Amy Emberling and Frank Carollo, 2017 (Chronicle Books)

Zingerman's Guide to Better Bacon, Ari Weinzweig, 2009 (Zingerman's Press)

Zingerman's Guide to Giving Great Service, Ari Weinzweig, 2004 (Hyperion Press)

MANAGEMENT

A Lapsed Anarchist's Approach to Building a Great Business (Zingerman's Guide to Good Leading), Ari Weinzweig, 2010 (Zingerman's Press)

A Lapsed Anarchist's Approach to Being a Better Leader (Zingerman's Guide to Good Leading), Ari Weinzweig, 2012 (Zingerman's Press)

BIBLIOGRAPHY

A Lapsed Anarchist's Approach to Managing Ourselves (Zingerman's Guide to Good Leading), Ari Weinzweig, 2013 (Zingerman's Press)

OTHER TITLES

Small Giants: Companies That Choose to Be Great Instead of Big, Bo Burlingham, 2005, updated 2016 (Portfolio)

The Toyota Way: 14 Manufacturing Principles from The World's Greatest Manufacturer, Jeffrey Liker, 2004 (McGraw-Hill Education)

Far Flung and Well Fed: The Food Writing of R. W. Apple Jr., 2009 (St. Martin's Press)

Acknowledgments

Satisfaction Guaranteed owes its existence to Irene Goodman, a Zingerman's fan, Michigan native, the holder of two degrees from the University of Michigan, and a much-respected literary agent. Out of the blue, Irene sent an email in fall, 2019, to see if I'd be interested in writing a Zingerman's book. Even though the pandemic created havoc in the literary world in 2020, Irene doggedly believed in this story and has been a cheerful enthusiast on my behalf.

I want to thank to team at Scribner, headed by my editor, Kara Watson, and editorial assistant Emily Polson. Thanks to Joel Holland for a wonderful cover illustration. Thanks also to production editor Dan Cuddy, marketing specialist Ashley Gilliam, publicist Abigail Novak, art director Jaya Miceli, designer Alexis Minieri, copy editor Martin Karlow, and the managing editorial team of Amanda Mulholland, Elizabeth Hubbard, and Annie Craig.

Ari Weinzweig and Paul Saginaw receive my sincere thanks and appreciation for allowing an outsider to tell their story. Along with them, I'd like to thank all the managing partners who made time for me, and the dozens of Zingerman's staff members and servers I've known at the Deli, Bakehouse, ZingTrain, Coffee, Creamery, Corman Farms, the Roadshow, and especially the Roadhouse. The staff there calls themselves my "second family," and my appreciation goes to Maria Lopez, Gaelan Campbell-

Fox, Zach Milner, Alex Rolfes, Bob Brunelli, Nancy Leat, Sharon Kramer, Chris Roberts, Mandie Carr, Kim Green, and Lisa Schultz. Everything you read about in here isn't just theory: I've seen it in practice. I've always felt welcome throughout ZCoB and loved their willingness to help me learn.

Among authors, chefs, Friends of Zingerman's, and others, my gratitude goes to Rick Bayless, Ti Martin, Alon Shaya, John T. Edge, Molly Stevens, Kat Gordon, Joanne Chang, Ina Pinkney, Stella Parks, Dorie Greenspan, Christine Cook, Richard Florida, Steve Wallag-Muno, Allen Leibowitz, and Audrey Petty.

I was so glad to have help from Colin Beresford and Alexa St. John as manuscript readers. I met and mentored both of them when they were editors at the *Michigan Daily*, and I'm so pleased to see how well they are doing in their journalism careers.

Thank you to my friends Marc Stewart, Luke Song, and Susan Kelley for their constant encouragement, and to my brother Frank Maynard, an enthusiastic Zingerman's fan who provided input along the way.

The late Nora Ephron was known for saying, "Everything is copy." In my case, every Zingerman's experience through the years—from crying in my pie class to figuring out flatbreads, wandering through the Deli, and watching the cooks and servers and front of the house staff doing their jobs at the Roadhouse—has gone into this book. I hope you'll enjoy it at least as much as a loaf of pecan raisin bread.

A NOTE ON SOURCING

The majority of material in this book was drawn from my original interviews, Zingerman's publications, and notes from previous interviews that I conducted through the years for a number of publications. Where quotes and information were drawn from other sources, I've noted that in the text.

Because of the independent operating structure of the ZCoB businesses, there are multiple versions of stories, varying dates, and different definitions, even across the Zingerman's websites. Or as numerous Zingerman's people told me, "No one remembers it the same way." This book makes a good-faith effort to share the most accurate information that I could find.

Micheline Maynard, Ann Arbor, Michigan

Index

INDEX